A School of the Prophets

A School of the Prophets

150 years of Spurgeon's College

Ian M. Randall

Foreword by Nigel G. Wright

First published in 2005 by Spurgeon's College

Spurgeon's College, 189 South Norwood Hill,
London, SE25 6DJ
www.spurgeons.ac.uk

British Library Cataloguing in Publication Data
A catalogue record for this book available from the British Library

ISBN: 009500682-1-7

Cover idea by Michael Roberts, design by Jonathan Rhodes
Printed in the UK by AE Simmons Ltd, Chelmsford

Dedicated to
the memory of
Martin J. Selman
(1947 – 2004)

Contents

Preface and Acknowledgements

Spurgeon's College staff and students meet for daily worship during term times and one day each week is devoted to praying for former students – members of what is called College Conference. Six of these are prayed for each week. They are written to beforehand so that they can send in news and requests for prayer, and for me it is one of the highlights of the week to listen to the letters and e-mails that we receive. Former students often speak about the influence that the College has had on their lives and how they value keeping in touch. It takes several years to complete the cycle of prayer for the people who have trained at the College.

As I have listened to many hundreds of letters it has struck me that in themselves they give a remarkable insight into the way in which ministry is being undertaken in this country and other parts of the world. Each person has a unique place within a bigger picture – one that I have tried to some extent to indicate in this book. It has been very difficult to pick out only some of the aspects of the story of Spurgeon's, since the story of each individual who has been part of the College, whether as staff or student, has its own significance.

The way in which the wider College network operates was illustrated after the terrible tsunami disaster of 26 December 2004, which left nearly 300,000 people dead, with millions of others homeless. Within a few days Clive and Ruth Doubleday, who were joint Presidents of College Conference for 2004/5, flew to Sri Lanka with aid channelled through their organization, Smile International. One of the first people they met was another member of College Conference, Kingsley Perera, General Secretary of the Baptist community in Sri Lanka. In reporting this, Clive spoke of the many other countries where he had similarly met College Conference members involved in ministry.

There is much more that will no doubt be written about C.H. Spurgeon and Spurgeon's College in the future, since there are extensive archives at the College with material waiting to be explored more fully. This book is not a complete history of the College. Rather, I have focused on themes that I consider have been crucial in the life of the College since it started a century and a half ago.

This book has been a collaborative venture. Judy Powles, the College Librarian, and Paul Scott-Evans, the College Business Manager, have been fully involved with me in the project and I want to pay tribute to their splendid work. I could not have produced this book without their involvement in a number of vital areas, such as the collection of material, the gathering and presentation of the illustrations, reading through the full text and the overseeing of the printing process.

Others have also helped me in various ways. Among these are former Principals of the College. Raymond Brown went through my manuscript in detail and his comments helped me greatly. I am indebted to Paul Beasley-Murray for reading the manuscript and for the time he spent with me. Michael Quicke, now in America, also read through the material and

I am grateful for his encouragement. Michael Roberts, a final year student commencing Baptist ministry in the summer in Huddersfield, very kindly produced the index. Others who have read through all or some of the chapters include the Principal, Nigel Wright, and other colleagues - John Colwell, Rachel Dutton, Debra Reid, Chris Voke and Roy Slack. Thank you. In addition I wish to thank Robert Amess, the current chair of College Council, and David Harper, his predecessor, both of whom read the whole manuscript. David and Doris Doonan, formerly missionaries with the Baptist Missionary Society in Brazil, helped me with the chapter on the international dimensions of the ministry of the College. Janice, my wife, reads all that I write and over the years has saved me from many errors – not only in my writing.

This book is dedicated to Martin Selman, who died in December 2004 at the age of 57, following a four year struggle with myeloma and leukaemia. Over the course of 29 years Martin served the College as a tutor, as Director of Research, Director of Postgraduate Studies, Academic Dean and Deputy Principal. He was a skilled linguist, who excelled in teaching Hebrew, Aramaic and Akkadian. Through his scholarship and deep theological insight, he brought scripture to life for generations of students. His scholarly work was extensive and Today's New International Version owes a considerable amount to him. Martin is greatly missed.

It has been a great pleasure for me to research and write this book about the College and to reflect again on its remarkable history. I have been made more deeply aware of the powerful vision that captivated C.H. Spurgeon in setting up and developing the training offered through the College. The College's work continues through its former students. As this book is published David Coffey, the General Secretary of the Baptist Union of Great Britain, who trained at the College in the 1960s, prepares to become President of the Baptist World Alliance; Kate Coleman, who trained in the 1990s, is President-elect of the Baptist Union – the first Black woman minister to be elected to the presidency; and David Doonan is due to become President of the BMS. I am grateful that I have had the privilege, since I began to teach here in 1992, of seeing the College's vision continuing to be worked out through men and women for whom Spurgeon's has been a part of their preparation for ministry.

Ian M. Randall
Easter 2005

Foreword

It is an enduring source of pleasure to me that the great majority of those who have trained for mission and ministry at Spurgeon's College look back upon the experience with thanksgiving and happiness. This is regularly impressed upon me by letters and conversations and strengthens my awareness that enterprises such as this thrive above all on the goodwill of many people. As the College comes to celebrate 150 years since its foundation in 1856 I am delighted that my colleague and deputy Dr Ian Randall has been able to do for us what he has previously done so well for others, to provide perspectives on the history of our own College so that others may understand something of what it has stood for.

A typical conversation I occasionally have concerns whether Spurgeon's College continues to uphold the beliefs and commitments of its Founder. The answer to this is both Yes and No. Times have changed, and Spurgeon certainly never envisaged a seminary in which students would study for university degrees and diplomas in the way they do now. Neither would he have anticipated the extent to which the College reflects the diversities of age, gender, denominational identity and ethnicity which make it such an exciting place to work. At the same time, this book demonstrates a remarkable consistency in the ethos and commitments of the College from the beginning until now. Warm-hearted evangelical faith, effective preaching and communication, evangelistic passion and church-planting, a global perspective and reach and an underlying current of joyful good humour, can all be detected as common elements throughout its history. These constitute the continuing agenda of this institution and, please God, always will do. Some of Spurgeon's most cited and most admirable words are his first at the Metropolitan Tabernacle:

> I would propose that the subject of the ministry in this house as long as this platform shall stand, and as long as this house shall be frequented by worshippers, shall be the person of Jesus Christ. I am never ashamed to avow myself a Calvinist; I shall not hesitate to take the name of Baptist; but if I am asked what is my creed, I reply, 'It is Jesus Christ.' My venerated predecessor, Dr Gill, has left a body of divinity admirable and excellent in its way; but the body of divinity to which I would pin and bind myself for ever, God helping me, is not his system, or any other human treatise; but Christ Jesus, who is the sum and substance of the gospel, who is in himself all theology, the incarnation of every precious truth, the all-glorious personal embodiment of the way, the truth and the life.

There is no doubt that like individuals, institutions have identities. Spurgeon's is a combination of at least three strands: there is a passionate evangelical faith, there are clear Baptist convictions concerning the church, its mission and its ministry, and there is a deeply rooted London context. Take any one of these away and you would be left with a different animal. The last of these strands is not insignificant as the College, which of course serves the whole nation and many parts of the world, has its existence amid the urban demands and changes of one of the world's oldest and greatest cities. The story of Baptists in this city, from the planting of the first Baptist church on English soil in Spitalfields in 1612 through to the new ethnic and linguistic communities that are regularly being established today, is a vibrant one, and in it Spurgeon played his strategic and celebrated part.

By the grace of God, the story this books recounts is one which is yet in its early stages and much more will yet to come to pass through this School of Prophets for the sake of God's kingdom and his glory alone.

Dr Nigel G. Wright, Principal of Spurgeon's College

Chapter 1: Introduction

Charles Haddon Spurgeon (1834-1892), the founder of what is now Spurgeon's College, was the most outstanding preacher of the Victorian era, a period that was marked by great pulpiteers who attracted large congregations. J.C. Carlile, a journalist and a Baptist minister trained at the College, who wrote one of the numerous biographies of Spurgeon, suggested that Spurgeon belonged to the category of people who at different periods in history 'have given a new expression of religion, and have turned the current of religious history into fresh channels'.[1] At the Metropolitan Tabernacle, situated at the Elephant and Castle, London, which was built for Spurgeon's congregation and which opened in 1861, Spurgeon regularly preached each morning and evening to over 5,000 people. Social ministries, notably an orphanage in Stockwell, were a feature of Spurgeon's ministry. During Spurgeon's pastorate at the Tabernacle over 14,000 people were baptised on profession of personal faith and joined the church membership. The sermons preached by Spurgeon also had a powerful international impact. By 1899 over a hundred million copies of his sermons had been produced, in twenty-three languages.[2] He was also a prolific writer. Spurgeon's robust Calvinistic theology was clearly conveyed by these means. He 'frankly admitted' in one of the College reports

Charles Haddon Spurgeon as a young man

Thomas Medhurst as a young man

that his views of the gospel and also his 'mode of training preachers' were out of line with much of the thinking prevalent in the 1850s.[3] It was his convictions about training that led him to found a College.

Founding and shaping a college

This book will not analyse the overall significance and influence of Spurgeon. It will look at only one part of Spurgeon's work – the College he set up to train pastors. The chapters that follow will analyse aspects of the vision for training that have characterised the College throughout its history. This introductory chapter will briefly trace the College's story - in particular its leadership - from Spurgeon onwards. Out of all Spurgeon's many endeavours, the College was, he insisted, his 'first-born and best beloved'. 'This is my life's work, to which I believe God has called me', he said on another occasion, 'and therefore I must do it. To preach the Gospel myself, and to train others to do it, is my life's object and aim.'[4] The College began as a result of Spurgeon's concern to train a young man, Thomas Medhurst, from Bermondsey, who was converted under Spurgeon's early London ministry at New Park Street Chapel (the Metropolitan Tabernacle was built because the numbers at New Park Street were so large) and was baptised in 1854. Medhurst began to preach in the open air and when two people joined New Park Street through his preaching Spurgeon suggested to Medhurst that he should prepare himself for pastoral work. He had then just finished his apprenticeship to a rope-maker and was almost twenty-one. Arrangements were made in July 1855 for Medhurst to stay with C.H. Hosken, pastor of Crayford Baptist Church, who lived at the Mill Road Collegiate School, Bexleyheath, Kent, and for him to study under the guidance of Spurgeon.[5] The origins of what became Spurgeon's College go back to 1855.

Spurgeon himself never went to a theological college. Soon after he began his first ministry, in the village of Waterbeach, Cambridgeshire, in 1851, he was strongly advised to enter Stepney College (later Regent's Park College), London. Believing that such training was useful, Spurgeon agreed to meet the eminent Baptist minister, Joseph Angus, who was the Principal of the College. Spurgeon described what took place:

> Dr. Angus, the tutor of the College, visited Cambridge, and it was arranged that we should meet at the house of Mr. Macmillan, the publisher. Thinking and praying over the matter, I entered the house exactly at the time appointed, and was shown into a room, where I waited patiently a couple of hours, feeling too much impressed with my own insignificance, and the greatness of the tutor from London, to venture to ring the bell, and make inquiries as to the unreasonably long delay. At last…the bell was set in motion, and on the arrival of the servant, the waiting young man was informed that the doctor had tarried in another room until he could stay no longer and had gone off to London by train. The stupid girl had given no information to the family that any one had called, and had been shown into the drawing-room….[6]

Not surprisingly, Spurgeon was disappointed, and thought of writing to apply to Stepney College. However, in the afternoon as he was walking to a village to take a preaching engagement he seemed to hear the words, 'Seekest thou great things for thyself, seek them not.' He took this as a sign not to pursue college studies. He did not doubt his own ability, commenting once that an educational mentor told him if he had studied for a degree

2

he could have won 'at a canter'.[7] In 1854 Spurgeon accepted the call to the pastorate of New Park Street Chapel, a historic Baptist church that had been in decline and then had 232 members. The way in which Spurgeon's ministry developed was due in part to what he termed the 'strange providence' of his non-meeting with Joseph Angus.[8]

Although Spurgeon began to teach Thomas Medhurst himself, it became clear that this was not a workable solution if the numbers being trained were to grow. Two of the New Park Street Chapel deacons, George Winsor and William Olney, promised Spurgeon financial help to extend the training, and he began to look for a suitable tutor. He talked the question over with Jonathan George, a Baptist minister in Walworth, who suggested George Rogers, then the pastor of the Independent (Congregational) Church, Albany Road, Camberwell. In Rogers, who had been pastor at Albany Road since 1829 and who during his ministry had given time to equipping himself theologically, Spurgeon believed he had found 'the very man I wanted'. Spurgeon described Rogers in 1870 as a man 'of Puritanic stamp, deeply learned, orthodox in doctrine, judicious, witty, devout, earnest, liberal in spirit'.[9] In the course of the ten years following its commencement the College (as Rogers noted in 1867) increased rapidly - from one student to between eighty and ninety. At that point it was reckoned that there were 150 people in ministry who had been trained at the Pastor's College, the name used at that time.[10] Spurgeon was the College President and was always known as 'the governor'. The studies initially took place in Rogers' own home, when the numbers involved were small, and after 1861 classes were held in basement rooms in the Metropolitan Tabernacle.[11]

Spreading influence

By the time Rogers wrote about the College in the mid-1860s it was considered by Rogers and others in the College's leadership that it was a widely-known institution and, more significantly, one 'adapted to the real wants of the age'.[12] Spurgeon noted that there had never been a shortage of suitable students, 'but on the contrary, a superabundance', and indicated that many applications were declined or the entry of students to the College was postponed.[13] The link with the Tabernacle was very important since a substantial proportion of the students and of the funds to support the College came from the Tabernacle congregation. Many of the early students had relatively little education and virtually no income. In 1870 the annual cost of running the College was about £5,000. This included providing financial help to the students with their living expenses and also the salaries of Rogers and his teaching colleagues. The needs of the College were made known in the Tabernacle's monthly magazine, *The Sword and the Trowel*. Almost £2,000 per annum for the College's expenses came from a weekly offering that was taken at the Tabernacle.[14] There were, however, other links which developed. The number of churches planted by those trained at the College was growing. It was reported in 1872 that over the preceding

Early tutors of the Pastor's College. Left to right: Archibald Fergusson, George Rogers, David Gracey, Frederick Marchant

C. H. Spurgeon with his brother James Archer Spurgeon

fifteen years 20,000 people had been added to the membership of churches where former students of the Pastors' College (from 1868 the title was changed from the original Pastor's College) were in ministry. The report in that year also noted that £1,700 had been donated at an annual dinner held for supporters of the College. Unexpected financial support also came from individuals.[15] The influence of the College was spreading significantly by the 1870s.

The next decade saw further changes. As the numbers of students grew, the basement rooms in the Tabernacle became increasingly unsuitable. The health of students was adversely affected because natural lighting was insufficient and gas lamps were burning all day. Money gradually came in for a College building and the foundation stone was laid in 1873. Spurgeon outlined the details of the building, situated in Temple Street, near the Tabernacle, on land purchased from the Ecclesiastical Commissioners. On the ground floor there was a large hall and a students' common room. On the first floor there was an assembly hall for conferences and also small classrooms. Many of the classrooms were used for Sunday School rooms on Sundays. Moveable partitions created flexibility. The Temple Street building was opened in 1874.[16] The College remained there until 1923 when it moved to South Norwood Hill. In 1881 David Gracey, the Classical Tutor at the College, took over the principalship from Rogers, who was by then over eighty. David Gracey, who was from a Presbyterian background in Northern Ireland, had begun studies at Glasgow University in 1859 with a view to entering Baptist ministry. In 1861 he heard C.H. Spurgeon preach in Glasgow and was so impressed that he applied for admission to the College. He soon became a tutor. Gracey, who was a fine Hebrew and classical scholar, was committed to the Calvinistic theology advocated by Spurgeon and also sought to encourage the kind of academic theological thinking which was, as he saw it, relevant to the task of communicating the gospel. Like Spurgeon, Gracey affirmed strongly that the College was founded for 'the masses'. The ministers who emerged from its training were 'emphatically men of the people'.[17]

Other tutors (who were termed Professors until the 1950s) assisted both Rogers and Gracey, while Spurgeon's brother, James Archer Spurgeon, ran the business side of the College, as well as being co-pastor of the Metropolitan Tabernacle and minister of the West Croydon Tabernacle. Archibald Fergusson, who came to London from Scotland in 1860 to teach at the College, had been affected by a revival in Dundee in 1839, in the church of which the famous Robert Murray McCheyne was minister. Fergusson served the College over three decades. Frederick Marchant, one of Spurgeon's earliest students, who had pastorates in Birmingham, Wandsworth and Hitchin, was appointed to the College in 1879 to teach classics and mathematics. In the 1880s Gracey taught Old Testament and theology. He was also pastor at New Southgate, but had to relinquish this when he was injured in a railway accident.[18] When Gracey died in 1893, at the age of fifty-three, Marchant became acting Principal, a role he fulfilled for five years. Archibald McCaig, another tutor who became Principal, was born near Perth, Scotland. Like Gracey, he was a Presbyterian who came to Baptist convictions. He soon engaged in open air preaching and remained an evangelist throughout his life. McCaig came to the College to train, serving as a pastor at Lewin Road, Streatham, and then in Brannoxtown, Co. Kildare, Northern Ireland. He gained the degrees of BA, LLB and LLD, and spoke eight languages. In 1892 he returned to the College as a tutor, becoming Principal in 1898, by which time Thomas Spurgeon, one of C.H. Spurgeon's twin sons, was College President. McCaig, who retired in 1925, insisted that the College maintained Spurgeon's own convictions, standing by 'the Old Flag held so nobly and tenaciously to the last by its beloved Founder'.[19] McCaig's devotion to C.H. Spurgeon was intense.

College Faculty c.1925
Left to right: James Taviner,
William Gaussen, Archibald McCaig (Principal),
Percy Evans

College Faculty 1956 with
Chairman of Council. Left to right:
Eric Worstead (Principal), Geoffrey Rusling,
Frank Fitzsimmonds, Stanley Dewhurst,
William H. Tebbit (Chairman of Council)

New developments

In 1923 the College moved to its present site in South Norwood, to a large house gifted to the College by the Hay Walker family, and the College's name became Spurgeon's College. Percy Evans, who joined the staff in 1922, took over from McCaig as Principal in 1925 and remained Principal until 1950. Evans trained at the College and between 1911 and 1925

College Faculty 1959
Left to right: Frank Fitzsimmonds,
Geoffrey Rusling, George Beasley-Murray
(Principal), Stanley Dewhurst

The 4 Principals in 2000 at the Thanksgiving
Service for Dr George Beasley-Murray. Left to
right: Michael Quicke, Paul Beasley-Murray,
Raymond Brown, Nigel Wright

had pastorates in Sutton Coldfield, Horley and Tonbridge. George Rogers had been Principal for twenty-three years, McCaig was at the College for thirty-three years, Gracey was a tutor for twenty-three years (fourteen of those as Principal), and Evans continued this tradition of long-term commitment to the College. In other ways, however, Evans led the College in new directions. As a residential community the College now mirrored more closely other theological colleges. Evans was keen to keep the College in the mainstream of evangelical and Baptist life. He also enhanced considerably the College's academic reputation, developing significant links with the University of London. Students were encouraged to seek to obtain a University degree. Evans himself received a DD from Edinburgh University for his work on baptism. Referring to 'innovations' in the academic sphere, the College report of 1949 noted that some regretted the changes that had been taking place at the College. In response, Evans and his colleagues were unapologetic: 'To these we say confidently that academics and evangelism march together. Culture and fervour are complementary. Degrees are not taken at the expense of the gospel.'[20]

The next two principalships were shorter in duration. Frederick Cawley, who was Principal from 1950 to 1955, came from a Brethren family. He trained at the College from 1909 to1912 and then served with the BMS in India and Trinidad. He subsequently had pastorates in Falkirk, Scotland, and in Camberwell and Penge, London. During his ministries he gained a BA and BD from London University and a PhD from Edinburgh, which was published as *The Transcendence of Christ* (1936), with a foreword by his supervisor, H.R. Mackintosh. From 1938 Cawley taught at the College, and as well as being noted for his bonhomie and enthusiasm he was regarded as someone who communicated 'the honour and dignity of the service of Christ'.[21] Frederick Cawley retired at the age of seventy and was followed as Principal by Eric Worstead, who had trained at the College and graduated in Arts and Divinity from London University. He held pastorates at Burnham-on-Crouch and Sydenham and then returned to the College in 1946 where he was a popular tutor and where his academic ability was evident. Eric Worstead's experience and range of gifts fitted him well for the principalship. In his own spiritual development, Worstead was helped through the Oxford Group, more commonly known by the 1940s as Moral Re-Armament (MRA), and as a consequence was guided, during his 'quiet time', to make adjustments in some of his attitudes to others. Worstead's personal assessment was that what had happened in his own spiritual life gave him a closer attachment to the Bible and to the Church's wider witness.[22] His association with MRA was not acceptable to the College Council, however, and his principalship came to an abrupt end.

Over the course of the next three decades Spurgeon's College benefitted from the post-war evangelical renaissance in Britain. George Beasley-Murray, who joined the staff in 1950, was committed to the evangelistic priorities that characterised the period from the 1950s onwards, exemplified not least by the Billy Graham campaigns. Beasley-Murray was a brilliant musician, an outstanding academic who gained a PhD in 1952 from London University, and an able pastor. He trained at the College, had pastorates from 1941 to 1950 at Ashurst Drive, Ilford, and then Zion Baptist Church, Cambridge, and after teaching at the College from 1950 to 1956 took a post at the Baptist seminary in Rüschlikon, Switzerland. When the Spurgeon's College principalship became vacant in 1957, Beasley-Murray was the only person considered for the post and his appointment was seen as one that would enhance the standing of the College. This proved to be the case. Beasley-Murray's combination of exacting scholarship and evangelistic commitment set the direction that the College would take over succeeding decades. When Beasley-Murray moved to the Southern Baptist Theological Seminary, Louisville, Kentucky, in 1973, as James Buchanan Professor of New Testament Interpretation, Raymond Brown succeeded him. Raymond Brown had trained at the College and had considerable pastoral experience, at Zion, Cambridge, for six years, and then for seven years at the large Upton Vale Baptist Church, Torquay. In 1966 the College's *Record* commented regarding Raymond Brown: 'It was clear, when he delivered his first sermon in the College sermon class, that he was destined for no ordinary ministry.'[24] Raymond Brown joined the College staff in 1971. As Principal, Brown, who had degrees from London and Cambridge Universities including a PhD and a Cambridge BD, both historical studies, continued the pastoral and the academic emphases at the College.

From the mid-1980s, as will be seen in more detail later, the patterns of training for ministry at Spurgeon's became much more varied. Significant changes were introduced by Paul Beasley-Murray (the son of George Beasley-Murray), who in 1986 followed Raymond Brown as Principal. After studying in Cambridge, at Northern Baptist College, at Manchester University, where he gained his PhD, and also in Zurich, Switzerland, Paul Beasley-Murray served with the BMS in Zaire and then had thirteen years as minister at Altrincham Baptist Church, Cheshire, where he saw substantial growth. When Beasley-Murray took up the principalship at Spurgeon's College he expressed his thankfulness for the 'proud evangelical and keenly evangelistic tradition' of the College. He saw the life of

Spurgeon's as colourful and varied, and traced these things back to the spirit of Spurgeon.[25] During the principalship of Paul Beasley-Murray, who wrote and spoke extensively in the area of leadership, the College developed significantly. The number of students doubled to 130 full time students. Church-based training expanded considerably and a church-based 'church planting and evangelism course' was launched. Beasley-Murray declared that this was 'going back to our roots'.[26] In 1992 Paul Beasley-Murray returned to pastoral ministry, at Central Baptist Church, Chelmsford.[27]

Both Michael Quicke, who was Principal from 1993 to 2000, and Nigel Wright, who followed him, encouraged the development of new training possibilities for a range of students, while continuing to emphasise that the central function of the College was to train people for ordained ministry. Michael Quicke was a student at the University of Cambridge and then trained for the ministry at Regent's Park College, Oxford. After working for two years as Secretary of the Baptist Students' Federation he had significant pastorates in Blackburn, from 1972 to 1980, and then at St Andrew's Street, Cambridge, from 1980 to 1993. Large numbers of people were attracted to St Andrew's Street during Quicke's ministry. Nigel Wright similarly had extensive pastoral experience. After studying at the University of Leeds, he trained at Spurgeon's and then had thirteen years of ministry at Ansdell Baptist Church, Lytham St Anne's, a period in which Ansdell experienced growth, became known as a congregation that participated in the charismatic renewal movement, and also planted other congregations. In 1986-7 Wright studied for an MTh at Glasgow University and then from 1987 to 1995 he was tutor in Christian doctrine at Spurgeon's. During this period he gained his PhD through King's College London. He then returned to the pastorate as senior minister at Altrincham Baptist Church, from 1995 to 2000, at which point he became College Principal. Under Michael Quicke's leadership Open Learning opportunities at Spurgeon's, which had developed during Paul Beasley-Murray's principalship, were given increased emphasis, as was training for preachers, and Nigel Wright introduced a new training course for evangelists. Wright's expressed vision, which was in line with that of Spurgeon, was for training 'attractive and evangelical ministers of the Gospel'.[28]

Conclusion

This introduction to the College and its leadership, from Spurgeon and George Rogers through the 150 years of the College's life, leads on to the examination in the chapters that follow of seven aspects of training that were important to Spurgeon and that have continued to be crucial in the life of the College – the training of pastors, a focus on evangelism, spiritual formation, links with the churches, opportunities for study, international dimensions, and the relationship of the College to evangelical life, including the impact of the Down Grade controversy. This book does not attempt to provide a comprehensive history of the College; rather it seeks to provoke thought about what is important in ministerial training. For those wishing to read more about the history, there are books about C.H. Spurgeon which include material on the College, such as J.C. Carlile's *C.H. Spurgeon: An Interpretative Biography*, W.Y. Fullerton's *C.H. Spurgeon: A Biography*, and more recently Patricia Kruppa's *Charles Haddon Spurgeon: A Preacher's Progress* and Lewis Drummond's *Spurgeon: Prince of Preachers*[29] In 1994, Mike Nicholls, who had been College Vice-Principal, produced *Lights to the World: A History of Spurgeon's College, 1856-1992*.[30] David Bebbington has a splendid chapter, 'Spurgeon and British Evangelical Theological Education', in *Theological Education in the Evangelical Tradition* (1996).[31] In 1950 the College *Record* suggested that the doom of Spurgeon's would be sealed if its story could be summarised as 'the fathers concerned themselves with the planting of orchards, and the sons were content to pass the apple sauce'.[32] Certainly the early decades of the College were characterised by remarkably creative innovation, and this book devotes considerable attention to those formative years. Within Spurgeonic circles the College was often known as 'a school of the prophets'.[33] The vision that motivated Spurgeon has had to be presented afresh and also renewed throughout the history of the College. This book explores the different ways in which the College has sought to continue to fulfil its early vision and to offer vocational training which will equip people to bring God's word to the world.

1   J.C. Carlile, *C.H. Spurgeon: An Interpretative Biography* (London: The Kingsgate Press, 1933), p. 30.

2   Ibid., pp. 236-7.

3   *Outline of the Lord's Work by the Pastors' College*, 1869 (London: Passmore & Alabaster, 1870), p. 4.

4   W.Y. Fullerton, *C.H. Spurgeon: A Biography* (London: Williams and Norgate, 1920), p. 227.

5   C.H. Spurgeon, *Autobiography; Compiled from his Diary, Letters, and Records by his Wife and his Private Secretary*. Vol.2 (London: Passmore and Alabaster, 1899, 4 vols.), p. 145.

6   *The Sword and the Trowel* [hereafter *S and T*], October 1865, p. 424. This was the monthly publication of the Metropolitan Tabernacle.

7   *S and T*, October 1865, p. 424; January 1881, p. 5.

8   *S and T*, October 1865, pp. 424-5.

9   *S and T*, April 1870, p. 146.

10   G. Rogers, 'An Outline of the Origin, History, Method and Success of the Pastor's College', in *Outline of the Lord's Work by the Pastor's College* (London: Passmore & Alabaster, 1867), pp. 19-20.

11   *S and T*, October 1865, p. 462; April 1870, p. 146.

12   Rogers, 'Outline', in *Outline* (1867), pp. 8, 10; cf. M.J. Quicke and I.M. Randall, '"The Real Wants of the Age": Spurgeon's College, London', *American Baptist Quarterly*, Vol. 18, No. 2 (1999), pp. 118-30.

13   *Outline* (1867), p. iv.

14   *S and T*, April 1870, p. 147.

15   *S and T*, May 1872, p. 240.

16   *S and T*, July 1873, p. 291; Fullerton, Spurgeon, p. 232.

17   *S and T*, June 1892, p. 278.

18   *S and T*, July 1892, pp. 421-3.

19   *Annual Paper Concerning the Lord's Work in Connection with the Pastors' College* [titles vary a little – hereafter AP], 1893-94, p. 10.

20   College *Annual Report*, 1949, p. 5.

21   *College Record*, August 1950, pp. 2-4.

22   Eric Worstead to the author, 10 June 1995. For the Oxford Group see I.M. Randall, *Evangelical Experiences* (Carlisle: Paternoster Press, 1999), chapter 9.

23   Minutes of the College Council, 13 December 1957.

24   *College Record*, June 1966, p. 9.

25   *College Record*, Winter 1986, p. 1.

26   *College Record*, Spring 1989, p. 1.

27   See P. Beasley-Murray, 'From College to Church: Reflections on Returning to the Pastorate', *Mainstream Newsletter*, No. 48, November 1993, pp. 4-6.

28   *College Record*, November 2000, p. 2

29   For Carlile and Fullerton see footnotes above. P.S. Kruppa, *Charles Haddon Spurgeon: A Preacher's Progress* (New York: Garland Pub., 1982); L.A. Drummond, *Spurgeon: Prince of Preachers* (Grand Rapids, Mich.: Kregel, 1992).

30   M. Nicholls, *Lights to the World: A History of Spurgeon's College, 1856-1992* (Harpenden: Nuprint, 1994).

31   D.W. Bebbington, 'Spurgeon and British Evangelical Theological Education', in D.G. Hart and R.A. Mohler, Jr., eds., *Theological Education in the Evangelical Tradition* (Grand Rapids: Baker Books, 1996), pp. 217-34.

32   *College Record*, December 1950, p. 15.

33   Spurgeon, *Autobiography*, Vol. 2, p. 141; cf. Fullerton, *Spurgeon*, p. 240.

Chapter 2: Producing pastors

Writing in the mid-1880s on the theme 'What we aim at in the Pastors' College', Spurgeon commented that there were many preachers who had considerable ability but who lacked the education and training to develop that further. The aim of the College, he said, had always been to seek to develop potential and to produce effective pastors. In this process he was determined that spiritual zeal should be encouraged rather than quenched. Those who came to College were those who felt 'a throbbing within them to preach' and Spurgeon had no interest 'in turning a rough-and-ready evangelist into a sapless essayist' through academic training.[1] For Spurgeon a number of elements were essential in College training: knowledge of the scriptures, of theology

Thomas Medhurst in later life

and of church history; study of language, including biblical and other languages, and a good general knowledge; the ability to communicate well in preaching; and awareness of how to conduct the work of the church.[2] Spurgeon looked to examples such as the Puritan, Richard Baxter, and his pastoral approach as summed up in his *Reformed Pastor*. 'Study successful models', said Spurgeon. 'I made [George] Whitefield my model years ago.'[3] The example of the development of Thomas Medhurst, the first of Spurgeon's students, was one that became legendary. Some people at New Park Street Chapel initially complained to Spurgeon about Medhurst's inadequate English. Spurgeon talked to Medhurst who said: 'I must preach, sir; and I shall preach unless you cut off my head.' The critics agreed then that he must preach.   This experience stimulated Spurgeon to provide preparation so that effective, educated pastors could be produced.

Knowledge of the scriptures

In 1874, in an address delivered to the College Conference - which drew together past and present students for a week each year - Spurgeon spoke about the need for ministers to have thorough biblical knowledge. He insisted that 'our main business is to study the Scriptures'. He encouraged pastors to use 'helps', such as commentaries, and considered that because many Christians now had access to this kind of reading material a greater challenge was presented to preachers. His view was that pastors had to be 'greater Biblical scholars' if they were going to be effective, and he advised them to 'keep in front of your hearers'.[5] Spurgeon was also concerned to counter eccentric, individualistic views of scripture. 'Plymouth Brethren', he said in an address to College students in 1869, 'delight to fish up some hitherto undiscovered tadpole of interpretation and cry it around town as a rare dainty. Let us be content with more ordinary and more wholesome fishery.'[6] He developed the same theme in his 1874 Conference address, emphasising the necessity of careful biblical interpretation and acquaintance with Christian tradition:

David Coffey, General Secretary of the Baptist Union of Great Britain from 1991

Nowadays, we hear men tear a single sentence of Scripture from its connection, and cry, 'Eureka! Eureka!' as if they had found a new truth; and yet they have not discovered a diamond, but a piece of broken glass. Had they been able to compare spiritual things with spiritual, had they understood the analogy of the faith, and had they been acquainted with the holy learning of the great Bible students of past ages, they would not have been quite so fast in vaunting their marvellous knowledge.[7]

But sound interpretation was not enough: the Bible had to come alive. On Friday afternoons Spurgeon came to speak to the students at the College, and as well as delivering lectures and discussing questions with the students, Spurgeon used some of those occasions to give students experience of engaging in and evaluating extempore preaching. Spurgeon instanced as the best thing of its kind the response of a student who had to speak on the word 'Zacchaeus'. He stood up and said, 'Mr. President and brethren, my subject is Zacchaeus, and it is therefore most appropriate to me; for first, Zacchaeus was little of stature, as am I; secondly, Zacchaeus was up a tree; so am I; thirdly, Zacchaeus made haste to come down; and so will I.' He then sat down. The students called to him to go on, but Spurgeon took the view that nothing could be added to such a perfect speech.[8] Although Spurgeon encouraged lively use of the Bible, he was determined that the College should teach students how to expound the Bible. 'Let us be thoroughly well acquainted with the great doctrines of the Word of God', he said, 'and let us be mighty in expounding the Scriptures. I am sure that no preaching will last so long, or build up a church so well, as the expository....if your ministries are to be lastingly useful you must be expositors.'[9]

This emphasis on biblical knowledge has been a continued feature of the teaching offered at the College. In the year 2000, David Coffey, who was General Secretary of the

Baptist Union from 1991 and who trained at the College under George Beasley-Murray, recollected the way in which Beasley-Murray gave priority to knowledge of the scriptures. David Coffey commented: 'Those of us privileged to be taught by George will never forget his lectures on John. They frequently took wings and underlined that George was never happier than when he was expounding scripture.' For Coffey, the strength of Beasley-Murray's work as a teacher was his ability to make his outstanding biblical scholarship available in plain language.[10] Beasley-Murray, as a particularly gifted teacher and as one of the leading New Testament scholars of his generation, set a standard. Among his more than twenty

College Faculty c.1972. Back row left to right: Rex Mason, Raymond Brown
Front row left to right: Frank Fitzsimmonds, George Beasley-Murray (Principal), Stanley Dewhurst

books were seminal works such as *Jesus and the Future* (1954), which was his doctoral thesis, and *Baptism in the New Testament* (1962), for which he received a Doctor of Divinity degree from London University. In an address that George Beasley-Murray gave to graduating students at the College in 1999, he urged the holding together of the strands that had claimed his life: evangelism and the study of the Bible.[11] By this time the College had developed a continuing fine reputation in the field of biblical studies through teachers in New Testament studies and biblical languages such as Frank Fitzsimmonds, John Maile and Alastair Campbell, and Old Testament scholars like Rex Mason and Martin Selman.[12] In the 1990s Martin Selman became internationally known for his work in the field of Bible translation.

Linked with this emphasis on biblical studies was a commitment to drawing from theological resources available through Christian thinkers of the past. 'Be well instructed in theology', Spurgeon urged, 'and do not regard the sneers of those who rail at it because they are ignorant of it. Many preachers are not theologians, and hence the mistakes which they make. It cannot do any hurt to the most lively evangelist to be also a sound theologian, and it may often be the means of saving him from gross blunders.'[13] Spurgeon opposed those who appeared to applaud ignorance. In the early twentieth century, however, although Spurgeon's Calvinistic theology was still espoused there was less liveliness in the theological teaching. Archibald McCaig, who was known for his inflexibility, reported that he had 'made no new discoveries in Theology or in Homiletics', but had enforced the old with as much freshness as possible.[14] One College student in the 1930s, G.J.M. Pearce, who later gained a PhD in theology at Aberdeen University and became a tutor at Regent's Park College, recalled hearing 'a very dull set of lectures on the atonement', apparently delivered (he surmised) because someone was worried that the students were not familiar with the doctrine of penal substitution, when in fact this was all they knew. There was an even duller set of lectures on baptism, which went on all year, and Pearce suggested that 'this mighty stream should be reduced to a small tributary'. There were no lectures on the Incarnation.[15] It was not until the later twentieth century, through theological tutors such as Bruce Milne, Nigel Wright and John Colwell, that the College gained a reputation for significant theological enterprise.[16] In the 1990s increasing numbers of students were engaged in study through the College for MTh, MPhil and PhD degrees in the biblical, theological and historical fields.

Language and literature

'The medium of conveying the truth', said Spurgeon, 'is language, and therefore we ought to know the nature, and rule, and form, and composition of language in general, and of our mother-tongue in particular.' Spurgeon linked the learning of Latin and Greek with good use of English. Speaking as he said 'with great deference to our Welsh brethren', Spurgeon suggested that English was 'the cream of other languages'.[17] This did not mean that a certain kind of elevated literary style was encouraged in the College. At times the reverse was the case. George Rogers explained: 'Literary attainments are not undervalued, nor discouraged, but opportunities and means are furnished for their acquirement. Instead, however, of being regarded as the chief object of ambition, they are pursued as means to an infinitely higher end.'[18] As David Bebbington puts it, the training 'was to be practical rather than literary, a down-to-earth affair rather than an imitation of Oxford or Cambridge.' Both C.H. Spurgeon and George Rogers opposed sophisticated modes of speech. 'The language of half our pulpits', Spurgeon pronounced in 1870, 'is alienating the working classes from public worship', and in typical style he stated: 'Now the devil does not care for your dialectics, and eclectic homiletics, or Germanic objectives and subjectives; but pelt him with Anglo-Saxon in the name of God, and he will shift his quarters.'[20] Rogers was adamant that students trained in the literature of the age were not the most effective ministers.[21]

Every encouragement was given, however, to the study not only of English but of Hebrew, Greek and Latin. Spurgeon believed that as higher levels of education became more general, preachers with limited knowledge would find it harder to obtain a hearing.[22] Each student should, therefore, seek to progress. Spurgeon advised one of his former students, T. Hancocks of Ramsgate: 'Never be satisfied with yourself, but go on growing, for we need men fitted to take the better positions, even more than we do the rank and file. Stick to your study even when you are in the midst of ministerial work, for you must be replenished continually or you cannot give out to others.'[23] Different courses of instruction were offered in the College, depending on ability. Someone who needed help with English was not required, said Spurgeon in 1871, 'to muddle his head with Hebrew'.[24]

Nonetheless, Spurgeon proudly noted that one student had come first in the competition for a respected Dr Williams's scholarship.[25] James Spurgeon, who had studied at Regent's Park College, was an able Syriac scholar. Flexibility within the overall training meant that the Pastors' College course, which was usually two years in the early decades (by contrast to four in other Baptist colleges), could be lengthened. When this happened it did not necessarily mean that more advanced study was taking place - it could signify remedial work. What Spurgeon aimed at was thorough linguistic skill, but he deplored ostentatious displays of literary knowledge. He commented in 1886: 'A brother who wishes to be thought highly cultured introduces German names: let him omit them. Another wishes to be thought great in the sacred languages…Mary Ann Jones is astonished, and so is Thomas Robinson in the gallery. *She* cannot read, and *he* cannot write.' Spurgeon pictured a 'good Christian woman' remarking: 'Greek is well enough, but I want the gospel.'[26]

The same priorities characterised David Gracey and Archibald McCaig. In January 1886 Gracey pronounced: 'In this College we do not put our trust in scholastic distinctions and academical honours; but in the Spirit of the Lord. While, therefore, you do all in your power to secure a sound reputation, we trust that you will place conspicuous emphasis on the unction of the Divine Spirit.'[27] The stress on 'unction', or spiritual power, was typically Spurgeonic. One former student, W.T. Soper, said that Spurgeon saw two things as necessary – 'gumption and unction'.[28] Gracey, who admired the American theologian, Jonathan Edwards (with his combination of scholarship and spiritual effectiveness), was adamant that no college or university could give 'unction' and insisted that without it the finest academic training would never make students 'fishers of men'.[29] In terms of the general educational background of the students, Thomas Spurgeon, as College President during McCaig's principalship, remarked in 1906 that students were probably better educated when they arrived at College than had been the case in his father's time. Also the course was longer than it had been in Spurgeon's day. Nonetheless, his commitment was to keeping 'absolutely unaltered' the College's educational principles.[30] Year after year McCaig took the students through A.A. Hodge's *Outlines of Theology* (1860); indeed the class was called 'the Hodge class'. Some former students, however, felt development was necessary. The College Committee on 11 June 1919 listened to the view of a deputation of younger ministers who had trained at the College. They appreciated what they had gained but suggested (in a 'respectful, kindly way', according to the minutes) changes to the curriculum and provision of post-collegiate courses.[31]

Under Percy Evans' leadership changes took place. It was recognised that the College could and should aim for higher levels of academic achievement. Evans himself became a Senator of London University. In the early 1940s a visiting speaker who revealed his indebtedness to a series of religious books published by Penguin was regarded as a little too populist, provoking one of the College lecturers to comment: 'In the Old Testament the man of God was fed by ravens, but I notice that you suggest the modern minister should

be supplied by Penguins.'[32] M.E. Aubrey, the General Secretary of the Baptist Union from 1925 to 1951, noted and applauded the changes taking place at the College. Speaking at the College in 1949, Aubrey, who admired the work of Percy Evans within the Baptist denomination, highlighted the way in which under Evans' principalship scholarship and evangelism were brought together. The College was sending out, he said 'the informed Evangelist and Evangelical'. Aubrey recommended that the students give themselves to a broad range of serious reading. He recommended the Puritan, Richard Baxter, and William Law, the author of *A Serious Call to a Devout and Holy Life*.[33] The stress on the best literature of the past was not at odds with C.H. Spurgeon's vision. Spurgeon ridiculed 'intellectual dandies' and with heavy sarcasm he commended '(t)hose superficial beings, the Puritans, and those unintelligent persons of the type of Jonathan Edwards and Andrew Fuller'.[34]

Ability to preach

In lectures he delivered to the College students on Friday afternoons (later published as *Lectures to my Students*), Spurgeon dealt with many aspects of preaching. The published lectures contained much helpful advice, as well as cartoon-style illustrations of preachers at work. In a lecture on 'Sermons – their Matter', Spurgeon argued for sermons that contained doctrine that was 'solid, substantial, and abundant'. However, he warned against giving attention to doctrinal problems that were not helpful to the hearers. The preaching of the cross was to be central. Issues such as 'the double procession' - a Trinitarian debate which divided the Eastern and the Western Churches - were 'of little concern to that godly woman, with seven children to support by her needle, who wants to hear far more of the lovingkindness of the God of providence than of those mysteries

profound'.[35] He urged students to think about the needs of their hearers: 'Why do ministers preach long sermons?', he asked. 'Is it for their own pleasure, or is it for the pleasure of the people?' At this point he did not think Puritan preaching could be copied.[36] Spurgeon also gave advice about choosing texts from which to preach. His method was to preach Christian doctrine from a variety of texts rather than preaching consecutively through

College students 1892-1896

books of the Bible. Although Spurgeon recounted many (often deliberately hilarious) examples of the bizarre ways in which texts were chosen, he still defended the principle as one that allowed for the guidance of the Holy Spirit.[37] This particular method of preaching from isolated texts is now rarely commended.

The way in which the communication of the biblical message took place was regarded by Spurgeon as of crucial importance. He often outlined key elements. The first was clarity. If preachers could not be understood, he suggested, it was probably because they did not themselves understand what they were trying to say. 'An average hearer', Spurgeon commented, 'who is unable to follow the course of thought of the preacher, ought not to worry himself, but to blame the preacher, whose business it is to make the matter clear.' Another necessity was a cogent style. It was important to be 'forceful'. For Spurgeon this did not mean speaking loudly. 'Nonsense', he remarked tersely, 'does not improve by being bellowed.' What he was advocating was good material that was delivered energetically. He also argued for preaching that was natural. 'I hope', he told his students, 'we have forsworn the tricks of professional orators, the strain after effect, the studied climax, the prearranged pause, the theatrical strut, the mouthing of words, and I know not what besides, which you may see in certain pompous divines who still survive upon the face of the earth.' He hoped that such preachers would become 'extinct animals' and that preachers would cultivate 'a living, natural, simple way of talking out the gospel'. Finally, he encouraged persuasiveness in preaching.[38]

Spurgeon told his students that he was surprised to see how little attention was given in the field of homiletics to the issue of obtaining and retaining the attention of hearers. This involved questions such as speed of delivery, repetition, use of illustrations, and length of sermons. 'Strike while the iron is hot', Spurgeon remarked in 1886, 'but do not keep on striking till the iron grows cold; though that is what many do.' He encouraged his students to say only as much as could be remembered. Spurgeon continued: 'Please remember, also, that your discourse is probably nothing like so precious to the people as it is to yourself.' As an illustration Spurgeon spoke about parents who look at their first child and feel that their baby is the finest born into the world. However, visitors asked to admire the baby may not all be as impressed as the parents. 'I have even known', Spurgeon commented, 'some of them hint that they had seen and heard quite enough of that delightful infant.' The students were warned not to make the same mistake with their sermons.[39] In a lecture entitled 'Attention!', Spurgeon recounted how a young man from the College had preached a long sermon to a village congregation. A farmer whose cows were waiting to be milked complained bitterly to Spurgeon that the sermon should have finished half an hour before it did and Spurgeon, agreeing with the farmer, suggested: 'The Society for the Prevention of Cruelty to Animals ought to have prosecuted that young sinner.'[40]

As well as hearing lectures on preaching, students were trained through having practical experience. Most preached in churches each week and on Monday mornings the senior students met with Spurgeon to evaluate their preaching experiences. Sermon plans were discussed and College sermon classes were held each week, at which students preached and their sermons were subject to thorough critique by staff and students. These much-dreaded events continued to be a feature of College life until the 1990s. Another way in which oratorical skills were developed was through weekly debates which involved staff and students. These took up topics proposed by the students. Opposing views were heard and the teaching staff normally had the last word. David Gracey wrote in 1891: 'Collisions of debate tend to widen the comprehension and to increase respect for the powers of others, if not always for one's own.'[41] The staff members were not always united in their views. In 1896 it emerged that Frederick Marchant, who was then acting Principal, held to 'universal atonement', the view that Christ died for all people, not solely for the elect.[42] Inevitably the debates that were convened tended, over a number of years (the minute books cover 1867 to 1917), to address the same ground. Topics discussed included the theory of evolution, unanswered prayer, the Plymouth Brethren, dealing with atheists, annihilation and eternal punishment, educational methods, total abstinence, capital punishment, the extent of the atonement, Puseyism, the second advent, spiritualism, faith healing, socialism, war, British Israelitism (the theory that the Anglo-Saxon races were descended from the 'Lost Tribes' of Israel and had a special place in God's purpose), Sunday closing of shops, revivals, musical instruments in worship, church government, Christian ministers and politics, smoking, the inspiration of scripture, the idea of Christian perfection, and foreign missions.[43]

The stress on effective preaching continued to be a central feature of the life of the College. During Percy Evans' period as Principal the basis of the College was often reaffirmed using Spurgeon's statement that the College existed to train 'attractive, impressive, effective preachers of the Gospel'. In 1936 Louisa Curtis of Rickmansworth founded a Lectureship in Evangelism and Pastoral Theology. In 1947 George Beasley-Murray spoke of Spurgeon's life-long aim, summed up in this statement: 'Of all I would wish to say this is the sum; my brethren, preach Christ, always and evermore. He is the whole Gospel.' Beasley-Murray was deeply impressed by how Spurgeon's sermons 'blaze with love for Christ and a yearning for his hearers to be saved'. Although Beasley-Murray had not then joined the College staff, the training of ministers was already in his mind. He considered that every student for the ministry should be made to read some of Spurgeon's sermons, and added – 'how I wish I had been!'[44] Later, as College Principal, Beasley-Murray continued to quote Spurgeon - 'preach Christ'.[45] In 1966 the American evangelist Billy Graham was leading a campaign in Britain, and in 1970 Graham visited the College. Against the background of the 1966 campaign Beasley-Murray stated: 'I have long felt that Spurgeon's greatest contribution to the Church is the example he set of preaching the gospel.' He then quoted Spurgeon: 'More and more I am jealous lest any views upon prophecy, church government, politics, or even systematic theology, should withdraw one of us from glorying in the cross of Christ...Your guess at the number of the beast...your conjectures concerning a personal Antichrist – forgive me, I count them mere bones for dogs... Blessed is that ministry of which *Christ is all!*'[46]

Pastoral practice

Although Spurgeon placed a very high value on preaching, the College also offered students training in pastoral practice. The College curriculum in the 1880s was heavily orientated towards biblical studies, doctrine, church history, languages and general knowledge, but the subject of the 'conduct of church work' was included.[47] One of the questions that Spurgeon was invariably asked by students was about pastoral visiting. His view was that a minister with only a small congregation in a country village would find it wise to do a good deal of pastoral visitation, not least so as to bring people into his congregation. Spurgeon was emphatic, however, that a minister who had a congregation of eight or nine hundred people could not go round all of them. 'It would be quite impossible for me to visit all my people', he observed, 'it would be absurd even to attempt it.' Even in answer to this question Spurgeon tended to emphasise the priority of preaching and of the study which that required. 'Keep your sermons up to the mark', he advised.[48] Spurgeon's own preference was for a larger church, and many of the students who left the College saw their churches grow significantly. This preference was influenced not only by mission considerations but also by Spurgeon's vision of expansive ministry. 'A large church', he once said, 'is to be preferred to a small one. The latter has many attractions, but it is not unlike a rowboat which a man is in danger of upsetting if he moves about, whereas the former is like an ocean steamer, on which he can parade without the possibility of upsetting the whole concern.'[49]

Yet Spurgeon did not envisage his students undertaking a ministry that was remote from the needs of the people whom they served. In 1881 Spurgeon commented in the College's annual report that the applicants to study at the College and become Baptist ministers 'are not tempted by rich livings, or even by the prospect of competent support; or, if they are, I take abundant pains to set before them the assured truth that they will find our ministry to be a warfare abounding in long marches and stern battles; but equally notable for meagre rations.'[50] The students stayed with members of the Metropolitan Tabernacle and soon discovered (if they did not know already) that their hosts were not wealthy people. Spurgeon regarded this as useful as it kept students in touch with 'the struggles and conditions of everyday life'.[51] The intention of the training at the College was to produce pastors who mixed with people easily. Spurgeon, in a lecture on 'The minister's ordinary conversation', recommended that ministers be sociable, not aloof.[52] In the context of a discussion of the ministerial office, Spurgeon was asked about applying the title 'Rev' to a Baptist minister. His answer was: 'If he is a very small mite of a man that no one could see except with a microscope, call him 'Rev'. If he is anybody that is anybody, you need not.'[53]

The College aimed to produce ministers that were hard-working. Spurgeon himself was a classic evangelical activist. In a celebrated passage he pronounced: 'Brethren, do something; *do something*; DO SOMETHING. While Committees waste their time over resolutions, do something. While Societies and Unions are making constitutions, let us win souls. Too often we discuss, and discuss, and discuss, while Satan only laughs in his sleeve. It is time we had done planning, and sought something to plan.'[54] Reporting on the progress of students at the College in the mid-1880s Spurgeon made clear his expectation that a minister trained at the College 'works harder than any other man in the parish' and told a tale of a pastor whose deacons complained about what they had to pay him since he did not get up until ten o'clock in the morning and was usually found in the garden smoking his pipe. Spurgeon wished the idler was in some other calling. His consolation was that the College had produced 'some of the most laborious [i.e. hardworking] and devout of men'.[55] Since this was the case, it was expected that the churches would pay a reasonable stipend. When C.T. Cook, who became the editor of the evangelical weekly, *The Christian*, settled in his first church, in 1913, McCaig insisted that the church pay him a stipend of not less than £120 per annum. At that point probably about a quarter of Baptist ministers in England had an annual stipend of under £100.[56] Dedicated ministers were viewed by the College as deserving proper support.

Finally, the College attempted to produce pastors who were leaders with vision and who could motivate others. Describing his personal motto, which became the motto of the College, *et teneo et teneor* ('I both hold and am held'), Spurgeon said: 'We labour to hold forth the cross of Christ with a bold hand among the sons of men, because that cross holds us fast by its attractive power.'[57] This involved leading worship, leading prayer meetings and church meetings, and giving leadership in mission. When Spurgeon was asked by students if ministers should take the whole of the Sunday services themselves he replied that given a choice it was his ideal for the minister to lead the whole service. In some congregations there might be a deacon who could do this. 'It is a misery', Spurgeon continued, 'to have the worship of God pulled to pieces as it has been in some places that I might mention, where one does a little portion, and someone else another part, and then at last the preacher is allowed to have his share of the proceedings.' Spurgeon's vision for worship was to have 'the whole service move forward towards one end'.[58] Ultimately, however, Spurgeon encouraged ministers to be people who mobilised their whole congregations, rather than undertaking all the tasks themselves. He pointed to the example of the community of Moravians in central Europe in the eighteenth century, who became a pioneering missionary agency. 'Look at the Moravians', urged Spurgeon, 'how every man or woman becomes a missionary, and how much they do for the Lord in consequence. Let us catch their spirit….It is not enough for us to say, "Those Moravians are very wonderful people." We ought to be wonderful people, too.'[59]

Models of ministry

Throughout the first half of the twentieth century the focus of training at Spurgeon's College was on preparing students for pastoral ministry. In 1951 Charles Johnson, then pastor at High Road, Ilford, and later Secretary of the London Baptist Association and chairman of College Council, recalled how he and his fellow-students during their time at College benefitted from lectures by Percy Evans. Through Evans' teaching, which was 'charged with spiritual purpose', they felt the high privilege of the pastoral office.[60] The courses that were followed and the degree examinations that were taken through London University, however, were in traditional academic subjects and thus did not reflect this concern for effective pastoral training. This was something that George Beasley-Murray and his teaching colleagues wished to address. Beasley's Murray's initial team was Geoffrey Rusling (Vice-Principal), who had studied at Spurgeon's and at Regent's Park College and then had a pastorate in Malvern before joining the College staff in 1951, Stanley Dewhurst, who after training at Spurgeon's had pastorates in Croydon, Selsdon, Ipswich and Wimbledon, and Frank Fitzsimmonds, who was a College student in the 1940s, was then pastor in New Malden, and for two years taught at Acadia University, Nova Scotia, Canada. Each of these was an experienced Baptist pastor, as was Rex Mason, who joined the staff later. Rex Mason had trained at Regent's Park College and served at the West Ham Central Mission, Upminister, and Albany Road, Cardiff.

George Beasley-Murray sought to make the system by which Spurgeon's students took external London University degrees work. In order to foster the university contact he agreed to be a London University examiner. In the early 1970s Beasley-Murray opened conversations with the Council for National Academic Awards (CNAA), established in 1964, to explore the development of a distinctive vocational degree - a BA which would fulfil the College's training needs. London Bible College (now the London School of Theology), the largest evangelical training college in Britain, was already pursuing this option and in 1972 thirty-nine LBC students enrolled for the new CNAA BA degree.[61] At Spurgeon's it was Raymond Brown, during his principalship from 1973 to 1986, who brought into being the new framework for training under the auspices of the CNAA. When Beasley-Murray moved to Louisville the members of the Spurgeon's College Council affirmed that they had in Brown, who was already on the College staff, the kind of person they were looking for to lead the College forward: a teacher of standing in his own field, someone whose personality and pastoral example could guide future generations, and someone who would connect well with the denomination.[62] The new BA commenced in 1974 and two years later full-time student enrolment had risen from fifty-three to seventy-five. It was recognised that the CNAA requirements meant increased administrative and academic workload.[63] Over the next decade, under Brown's leadership, the academic life of the College was significantly reshaped.

College Faculty c.1978. Back row left to right: Peter Manson, John Maile, Bruce Milne, Martin Selman, Michael Nicholls
Front row: J.J. Brown, Stanley Dewhurst, Raymond Brown (Principal), Frank Fitzsimmonds

Full-time tutorial staff at the College increased in the 1970s to meet the new demands: in the Old Testament field Martin Selman, who was then beginning his academic career, replaced Rex Mason, who had moved to Regent's Park College; Bruce Milne, who had trained at the College in the 1960s and had been in pastoral ministry in Scotland, joined the staff and taught Christian Doctrine; Brian Stanley, who became a leading historian in the field of mission studies, was appointed as Academic Registrar and Librarian; and Peter Manson, who had trained at the Baptist College in Cardiff and who had been a minister in Cardiff and then at Woolwich Baptist Church, became the tutor in Pastoral Studies and Evangelism. John Maile, who had trained at the College and had been at Old Lodge Lane, Purley, became a Research Fellow in New Testament in 1974, and a tutor in 1979. Stanley Dewhurst, a full-time tutor since 1955, served as part-time librarian.[64] The CNAA degree had three strands - biblical, theological-historical and contextual – which were studied over three years to obtain a BA, and in addition the College introduced a fourth year which was exclusively devoted to pastoral studies, under the leadership of Peter Manson. In 1976 Raymond Brown outlined his plans for a new Pastoral Studies Centre.[65] The fourth year course was designed 'to equip a student in a practical way for the Christian ministry'.[66] Part-time church-based courses leading to the Cambridge Diploma in Religious Studies or, for some students, to a degree, developed from 1976 under the direction of Mike Nicholls, who had trained at the College and had been minister of Alder Road, Parkstone. With the growth in courses and student numbers came the need for additional library facilities - something which was also a priority for the CNAA - as well as the need for extended College accommodation.[67]

Further important developments took place in the 1980s and 1990s. The closure by the government of the CNAA meant that new accreditation was necessary and from 1992 the College's degrees were validated by the University of Wales. Paul Beasley-Murray developed the vocational nature of the CNAA degree and also church-based training, in which students spent half of each week in study and half in church work. This was a highly significant development, with the church-based model becoming the predominant mode of training. The church-based model was already being used at Northern Baptist College and at Regent's Park College, where Bruce Keeble, who trained at Spurgeon's in the 1950s, directed pastoral studies. The importance of church-based pastoral and mission studies was indicated by the appointment to the College staff of Robert Archer, who had wide pastoral experience, and Stuart Christine, who had considerable missionary experience. Peter Manson became South Wales Area Superintendent and was succeeded at Spurgeon's in 1992 by Bill Allen, who had trained at the College in the 1970s and who was an Industrial Chaplain with Teeside Industrial Mission. Allen conducted a survey, asking church members what qualities made for 'good' leaders. Bill Allen's work drew on ideas from John Adair's 'three-circle' model, which had also been used by Paul Beasley-Murray, from a Methodist report, 'The Ministry of the People of God in the World', and from Bethel Theological Seminary, USA. The model brought together three overlapping areas: first 'knowledge', the aim in this area being to encourage informed biblical and theological convictions; second, 'character and spirituality', to do with Christian qualities in the person being trained; and, third, 'skills', involving at how students communicate, build teams and nurture communities.[68] These elements were covered in the modules delivered by the College.

Conclusion

As indicated by its name, the Pastors' College, the focus of the training offered at the College has always been vocational. This is central to the idea of a 'school of the prophets'. As Spurgeon looked back in 1870, he spoke of being led to take a few young men, such as Thomas Medhurst, with some experience of preaching, and put them under the supervision of 'some able minister' – George Rogers, as it transpired - 'so that he might train them in the Scriptures, and in all other knowledge helpful to the understanding and proclamation of the truth'.[69] The emphasis was thoroughly practical. The College never claimed to be able to take anyone and turn that person into a pastor: there had to be evidence of ability in preaching, leading and dealing with people. Spurgeon stated that the College 'aims to keep out of the sacred office those who are not called to it. We are continually declining candidates because we question their fitness'. Those accepted had a clear call, some evidence of gifting, and a willingness to learn.[70] This vision for vocational training continued. In language reminiscent of Spurgeon, George Beasley-Murray stated (at a time when there were no female students) that he had 'striven to help my students to be men of God and men of the Word'.[71] Developments from the mid-1970s under Raymond Brown gave greater coherence to the training of pastors. The College gained from CNAA validation of vocational training. In 1989 George Beasley-Murray was awarded a CNAA honorary DLitt. At the core of the College from its beginning has been a desire for the gospel to be communicated. In 1998 Michael Quicke, Principal from 1993 until 2000, when he became C.W. Koller Professor of Preaching, Northern Baptist Theological Seminary, Chicago, stressed the preaching tradition of the College. Announcing a partnership with the College of Preachers, directed by Stephen Wright, an Anglican scholar, Michael Quicke said: 'For us at Spurgeon's preaching the Word has always been at the heart of our mission. It was for the equipping of preachers that C.H. Spurgeon first had the vision for this work.'[72]

1 *AP*, 1886-87, pp. 3-4.

2 Ibid., pp. 5-9.

3 Fullerton, *Spurgeon*, p. 235. George Whitefield was a pioneering leader and an outstanding preacher in the eighteenth-century Evangelical Revival.

4 Spurgeon, *Autobiography*, Vol. 2, p. 151.

5 *S and T*, May 1874, p. 221. This address was later published in C.H. Spurgeon, An *All-Round Ministry* (London: Passmore and Alabaster, 1900), pp. 40-66.

6 *S and T*, July 1869, p. 301.

7 *S and T*, May 1874, p. 221.

8 Fullerton, *Spurgeon*, pp. 237-8.

9 *S and T*, May 1874, p. 221.

10 *College Record*, June 2000, p. 5

11 P. Beasley-Murray, *Fearless for Truth: A Personal Portrait of the Life of George Beasley-Murray* (Carlisle: Paternoster Press, 2002), p. 111.

12 See, for example, R. Mason, *Preaching the Tradition: Homily and Hermeneutics after the Exile* (Cambridge: CUP, 1990); M.J. Selman, commentary, *1 and 2 Chronicles* (Leicester: IVP, 1994); R.A. Campbell, *The Elders: Seniority within Earliest Christianity* (Edinburgh, T & T Clark, 1994).

13 *S and T*, May 1874, pp. 221-2.

14 *AP*, 1907-8, p. 5. Unfortunately Lewis Drummond misses out McCaig's long principalship completely, stating that David Gracey was succeeded by Percy Evans: Drummond, *Spurgeon: Prince of Preachers*, p. 419.

15 *College Record*, May 1955, pp. 7-12.

16 See, for example, B. Milne, *Know the Truth: A Handbook of Christian Belief* (Leicester: IVP, 1982); N.G. Wright, *Disavowing Constantine* (Carlisle: Paternoster Press, 2000); J.E. Colwell, *Living the Christian Story: The distinctiveness of Christian ethics* (Edinburgh: T&T Clark, 2001).

17 *AP*, 1886-87, pp. 7-8.

18 Rogers, 'Outline' in *Outline* (1867), p. 10.

19 Bebbington, 'Spurgeon and British Evangelical Theological Education', pp. 219-20.

20 *S and T*, April 1871, p. 218; cf. AP, 1870, pp. 5-6.

21 *S and T*, January 1866, p. 42.

22 *AP*, 1881-82, p. 6.

23 Carlile, *Spurgeon*, p. 181.

24 *S and T*, April 1871, p. 226.

25 *S and T*, April 1873, p. 147.

26 *S and T*, February 1886, p. 53.

27 Reported in *S and T*, January 1897, p. 31.

28 *S and T*, October 1903, p. 512.

29 Reported in *S and T*, January 1897, p. 31.

30 *AP*, 1905-6, pp. 4-5.

31 Minutes of the College Committee, 11 June 1919 (Box 14); cf. Nicholls, *Lights to the World*, p. 125.

32 *Spurgeon's College Magazine*, Midsummer 1943, p. 25. This was retold: *College Record*, December 1950, p. 15.

33 *College Record*, September 1949, pp. 2-3.

34 *AP*, 1870, p. 9.

35 C.H. Spurgeon, *Lectures to my Students: First Series* (London: Passmore and Alabaster, 1906), pp. 72-8.

36 *S and T*, February 1886, p. 49.

37 Spurgeon, *Lectures to my Students*, p. 90.

38 *S and T*, May 1874, pp. 224-5; Spurgeon, *All-Round Ministry*, pp. 50-2.

39 *S and T*, February 1886, pp. 50-2.

40 Spurgeon, *Lectures to my Students*, pp. 144-5.

41 *S and T*, May 1891, pp. 263-4.

42 Minutes of the College Committee, 20 July 1896 (Box 14).

43 Nicholls, *Lights to the World*, pp. 73-4; Minute books, 1867-1917 (Box 6).

44 *Spurgeon's College Magazine*, Autumn 1947, pp. 3-4.

45 *College Record*, June 1964, p. 3.

46 *College Record*, June 1966, p. 18.

47 Nicholls, *Lights to the World*, pp. 68-9.

48 *S and T*, May 1897, p. 206. This was a report of questions asked Spurgeon at his home, Westwood. Students would gather in the garden, under the 'Question Oak'.

49 Fullerton, *Spurgeon*, p. 236.

50 *S and T*, June 1881, p. 302; AP, 1880-81, p. 4.

51 C.H. Spurgeon, 'Concerning the Pastor's College', in *Outline*, 1869, pp. 7-8.

52 Spurgeon, *Lectures to my Students*, p. 182.

53 *S and T*, July 1897, p. 367. Report of questions to Spurgeon.

54 Spurgeon, *All-Round Ministry*, p. 63.

55 *AP*, 1885-86, p. 29.

56 *College Record*, June 1963, p. 4.

57 Spurgeon, *Autobiography*, Vol. 2, p. 150. For the hymn-writer Dora Greenwell and the origins of the motto, see C.L. Maynard, *Dora Greenwell* (London: H.R. Allensen, n.d.).

58 *S and T*, February 1897, p. 51

59 Spurgeon, *All-Round Ministry*, p. 66.

60 *College Record*, August 1951, pp. 4-5.

61 See I.M. Randall, *Educating Evangelicalism: The Origins, Development and Impact of London Bible College* (Carlisle: Paternoster Press, 2000), pp. 170-1, 202.

62 Minutes of a Special Meeting of the College Council, 27 July 1973.

63 Minutes of College Council, 2-4 April 1975.

64 Nicholls, *Lights to the World*, p.176.

65 *College Record*, June 1976, p. 4.

66 *College Record*, December 1978, p. 25.

67 See Appendix 1 by Judy Powles.

68 W.J. Allen, 'Pathways to Leadership: The provision of education and training for leadership in the ordained ministry', University of Wales PhD thesis (1999).

69 *S and T*, April 1870, p. 146.

70 *S and T*, May 1887, p. 206.

71 *College Record*, June 1958, p. 2.

72 *College Record*, April 1998, p. 2.

Chapter 3: Enabling evangelism

Evangelism was integral to C.H. Spurgeon's conception of ministry. A concern to equip people to 'preach the gospel', as Spurgeon often put it, characterised the ethos of the College in its early decades and continued thereafter to be a feature of the training the College offered. When Spurgeon began the College it was, he related, because he was in contact with a group of 'earnest young men' who had come to Christ under his ministry and who 'felt an irresistible impulse to preach the gospel'. He recognised that they lacked education, and that this could be a serious problem, but he did not want to suppress their evangelistic zeal. In any case, he realised that if he had tried to stop these budding evangelists 'they would respectfully but conscientiously have ignored my recommendation'. With this in mind, Spurgeon committed himself, through the College, to giving those with what he saw as an evangelistic as well as a pastoral calling 'an opportunity to educate themselves for the work'.[1] Again Thomas Medhurst is a prime example. His preaching in the open air was his first attempt at ministry, his initial training led to his call as temporary pastor of the Baptist Church at Kingston-upon-Thames in 1856, and in the meantime he continued his studies under George Rogers.[2] During Medhurst's pastorates – Kingston, Coleraine in Ireland, Glasgow, and Lake Road, Portsmouth - he baptised nearly a thousand people.[3] The College's annual report of 1884-85 re-affirmed that its purpose was to educate those called by the Holy Spirit to witness for Christ in order to 'maintain and spread the gospel of the grace of God'.[4]

Forming new congregations

In the first few decades of the College's life 'the spread of the gospel' took place to a large extent through students from the College starting new Baptist congregations. In the 1868 College report Spurgeon commented that 'a very large proportion of our brethren have *created their own spheres*, and others have accepted pastorates where the prospects were such as to repel all others.'[5] This phenomenon continued, and in 1881 Spurgeon expressed his enthusiasm in this way:

> It is my greatest pleasure to aid in commencing new churches. The oftener brethren can create their own spheres the more glad shall I be. It is not needful to repeat the details of former reports; but many churches have been founded through the College, and there are more to follow. I announced at the beginning of this enterprise that it was not alone for the education of ministers, but for the general spread of the Gospel; and this has been adhered to, a part of the income being always expended in that direction.[6]

At the time of Spurgeon's death in 1892, the number of students who had been trained at the Pastors' College numbered 863, and 627 of them were serving in the Baptist denomination as pastors, missionaries and evangelists. More than 90,000 people had been baptised in churches led by former students at the College. Over half the new churches founded within the denomination in the period 1865 to 1887 were as a result of the activities of Spurgeon and the students of the College.[7]

There was a particular focus on starting congregations in London, with talk in 1866, after the College had been in operation for a decade, of 'new and flourishing churches' having been founded.[8] Spurgeon, who was always specific about results, was delighted to report in that year that in the London area eight new Baptist churches formed under the leadership of former College students had acquired or built chapels. In ten other cases Baptist churches had been formed which did not yet have their own buildings. In seven other instances preaching was being carried on with a view to founding churches.[9] These churches were growing quickly, with membership increasing on average by at least 20% per annum. This growth rate was reckoned to be twice the national average for Baptist churches of the time. In 1867 the average church led by a minister trained at the College had 118 members.[10] Not all the church plants survived, but Spurgeon's calculation in 1873 was that forty-five churches in the London area had been planted as a result of the College's work, with the aid of individual friends and the London Baptist Association (LBA).[11] The Baptist Union was itself expanding and it was not only Spurgeon who was involved in church planting. But the churches associated with the College were being led by young, confident ministers, who were expecting success, and the churches took on something of this ethos.[12] Between 1865 and 1886 membership of LBA churches increased by 28,308, nearly two-thirds of this growth being attributable to 'Spurgeon's churches'.[13]

Often starting a congregation meant meeting initially in a hired building. Spurgeon encouraged this as a first step. Not all these pioneering efforts were successful, but many became established Baptist churches. Outreach which began in Wandsworth in 1859, for instance, brought into being East Hill Baptist Church. Under John W. Genders, who had become a student at the College a year earlier and who later undertook teaching at the College, meetings were started in the Assembly Rooms of the Spread Eagle Tavern. By the mid-1860s the membership was over 150 and a chapel was erected costing £3,000.[14] An inn was also used as a venue in Bromley, Kent, where meetings were started in 1862 in the Assembly Rooms of the White Hart. Archibald G. Brown, aged nineteen and a student at the College, saw the Bromley congregations grow from about 30 to 200 in a year. In 1863 a church was formed with twenty members and two years later it was reported that a large chapel was being erected.[15] A.G. Brown became one of Spurgeon's closest associates. The East London Tabernacle, Stepney Green, which became the second largest Baptist church in London (after the Metropolitan Tabernacle), met in the Beaumont Hall, Mile End Road. Students from the College, first Joseph Harrison and then Thomas Ness (from

Edinburgh), built the East London Tabernacle up to 200 people in the early 1860s, and a chapel seating 800 was erected in 1864. When Ness left to go to Australia the church asked Spurgeon for advice about the pastorate. He recommended A.G. Brown, commenting that he would willingly walk four miles any day to hear Brown preach. Brown was duly called and under his ministry Sunday evening congregations (which in churches

The East London Tabernacle, Stepney Green

of this period were always larger than Sunday morning congregations) grew to 1,200 people and by 1868 the rapidly-growing membership had reached 500.[16]

In all these cases attention was quickly focussed on having a permanent building. The later 1860s saw new causes in places such as Battersea, Brixton, Ealing, Camberwell, Greenwich, Deptford, Cheam, Brentford, Stratford, Clerkenwell, Holloway and Streatham, with each obtaining or seeking to build chapels. In Vauxhall a church building that had been vacated by a high Anglican congregation was able to be secured. Spurgeon himself would often supply part of the money needed to build or purchase chapels and in some cases wealthy individuals offered substantial help. Building work invariably brought challenges. In 1867 *The Sword and the Trowel* noted that at Penge, in south London, the work of establishing a congregation was progressing 'under the energetic care of Mr. M. Cox, one of the students of our College, to whose indefatigable labours this church owes its origin and rapid growth', but reported that a gale had seriously damaged the chapel which was being built. The report continued: 'Funds are gradually coming in, but a great effort will be needed if the house is to be opened free of debt….Penge is a rapidly increasing suburb: the new chapel will stand in the midst of a large working population.' Building churches in developing suburbs was strategic. It was noted that as part of the building fund efforts in Penge there would be 'a Bazaar in the building, in the Easter week, and Mrs Spurgeon, who is the President of the Ladies' Committee, will be very much obliged to friends who will send help'.[17]

As well as pioneering new churches, students from the College were involved in reviving existing Baptist causes. When C.B. Sawday, a student who was a member of the Metropolitan Tabernacle, went to Vernon Chapel, King's Cross, in 1863, the chapel was almost empty. After three and a half years it was over-crowded, with conversions reported every week. 650 people had applied for membership.[18] In order to allow the chapel to be extended the congregation temporarily moved out of the building and used a large gymnasium seating 2,300.[19] Sawday remained at Vernon for twenty-five years. John Wilson, at the Woolwich Baptist Tabernacle, had a considerably longer ministry. Wilson, a friend of Archibald McCaig, came from Scotland to train at the College and began his

J. Manton Smith and W.Y. Fullerton

ministry in Woolwich in 1878, when the membership of the church was ninety, and by the early twentieth century the church had almost 1,500 members, with a further one thousand in attendance, including children. Wilson was a much-loved pastor and he was elected only the second Freeman of the Borough of Woolwich.[20] Former College students also sought to revitalise churches that were in decline outside London, for example in Tonbridge, in Kent, and in South Shields and Middlesbrough in the North-East. In some cases groups of Baptists sought a student from the College. In Burnley, Lancashire, for instance, some friends wanted to establish a Baptist church and applied to Spurgeon for a student. G.W. Oldring, who entered the College in 1866, was chosen. Although initially the church was formed with fifteen members, a room was hired accommodating 300-400 people and this was opened for worship in 1868.[21] In most cases the expectation that growth would take place was fulfilled.

Utilising evangelists

Spurgeon described the College in 1873 as a 'Home Missionary Society for the spread of the gospel'.[22] The Tabernacle functioned in the same way, with an Evangelists' Association of seventy members that provided training in areas such as visiting and public speaking. Spurgeon considered that proper delivery in speaking had often been passed over by universities as 'beneath notice', but it was a professional skill.[23] Linked more directly with the College was 'The Pastors' College Society of Evangelists', which began in the 1870s and was designed to further 'mission work in our own country', as W.Y. Fullerton (the leading evangelist with the Society in the 1880s) put it. In 1874 William Higgins left College and joined the newly-formed Society – an event heralded by the announcement that the 'earnest evangelist Mr Higgins is ready to visit the churches' – and later in the 1870s two evangelists who both trained at the College, W.Y. Fullerton and J. Manton Smith, were in great demand. Although Fullerton, an Irishman, was the leader, this was a joint ministry, parallelling in part that of D.L. Moody and Ira Sankey. Fullerton described how Smith's 'Gospel witness, singing, and cornet-playing were renowned all over the kingdom and beyond'.[24] A report in *The Sword and the Trowel* in 1881 highlighted how the College Society's evangelists had 'traversed the land with great diligence and the Lord has set His seal to their work'.[25] Among the other evangelists were John Burnham, a preacher/singer, and W.J. Taylor and J.G. Williams, who later joined the interdenominational Evangelisation Society.[26]

The evangelists worked with many denominations, to some extent taking on the approach of D.L. Moody. In 1884 the College students went to hear Moody preach in Croydon and Spurgeon commented: 'We are more and more impressed with a sense of the remarkable power which rests upon the beloved Moody.'[27] Whereas those students who were planting churches had a clear denominational agenda – their task was to establish Baptist congregations - a Society of Evangelists' report covering 1890-91 noted that the evangelists had served not only with Baptists, but also with Congregationalists, Presbyterians, Methodists and the Society of Friends. There had also been missions to young people connected with YMCAs and YWCAs. In many places hundreds had professed conversion.[28] At Regent's Park Chapel, London, where F.B. Meyer (the leading Baptist speaker at the Keswick Convention) was pastor, Fullerton and Smith held a campaign in 1891. At a Chapel

FULLERTON AND SMITH
ARE
COMING TO THE METROPOLITAN TABERNACLE,
November 18th to the 24th, 1889.
HELP THEM!

DEAR FRIENDS,

I am most anxious that a great many should be saved during the Special Services which are to be held by Messrs. FULLERTON & SMITH. Hence I invite YOU to be present, if you are yourself undecided. Who can tell what blessing is in store for you ! "Faith cometh by hearing, and hearing by the Word of God." It may be that in hearing your soul shall live.

If you are on the Lord's side already, I would entreat you to bring in others, that the house may be filled. The people must first be brought within hearing, and then we must pray the Holy Spirit to bring them within feeling, and then within the faith-look of Jesus. Our dependence is upon the power of the Holy Ghost; but we do really believe that he is able to do exceeding abundantly above what we ask, or even think. Preaching the gospel is the means which he is pleased to bless. Pray much that he may work by the means of our Evangelists, and bring thousands to the Lord Jesus. They are men full of faith and of the Holy Ghost, and God is with them.

Come yourself! Come often! Come to every service, if you can! Each time bring some two, or more, strangers. The more strange they are the better; for then they are not gospel-hardened. Get round you a little band of sinners, for whom you are anxious that they should be saved. Come up to the Services with them in a prayerful spirit. Expect that God will save them.

I shall be far away : but my heart will be with you at every service, and I shall be hungering to hear that you have a blessing. I lay this charge upon every friend I have : be in earnest, that our excellent and earnest Evangelists should not labour in vain.

Begin at once to canvass the neighbourhood. Speak to individuals. Wake up the indifferent. By the love of our Lord Jesus, I entreat you, men and brethren, help!

Yours, for Christ's sake,

C.H. Spurgeon

The Evangelists will be at the Metropolitan Tabernacle from Nov. 18th to Nov. 24th. Sunday Services at 11 a.m., 3 p.m., and 6.30 p.m.; Week Evenings at 8.

Leaflet from C.H. Spurgeon encouraging attendance at a Fullerton and Smith evangelistic meeting

members meeting Meyer announced that many 'backsliders' had been affected and others had come to faith in Christ. During that year the Chapel, which had a unique ministry in the West End of London, welcomed eighty-two new members by profession of faith.[29] The Earl of Shaftesbury, the most prominent evangelical social reformer in the nineteenth century, was enthusiastic about the College evangelists he heard at services in theatres. He noted their colloquial way of addressing the people. Shaftesbury, an evangelical Anglican, had no faith in high church ritual - 'bits of wax candle' and 'gymnastics in the church' – but applauded the evangelistic work of 'the pupils trained in Mr. Spurgeon's College'.[30] It was noted in 1891 that College evangelists had not preached in any Anglican church, Salvation Army corps, or Brethren meeting room. Nonetheless, Fullerton referred to the way they functioned as being 'truly Catholic; not undenominational, but inter-denominational'.[31]

There were, however, some within Baptist circles who questioned the value of evangelists. In 1881 Fullerton wrote with a degree of bitterness: 'We magnify our office; not, we trust, above what it deserves, but above what it is generally supposed to include. Indeed, it is amusing sometimes to notice the suspicion and prejudice and hostility with which the name... [evangelist] is greeted. "He is an evangelist!" Let us avoid him, and hamper him, and hinder him!'[32] Fullerton argued that evangelists should be trained, organised and should work for and with the churches, and he even suggested a form of covenant that would bind pastors and evangelists together. 'Evangelist, "Will you have the pastor to be your co-worker…?" Pastor, "Will you welcome this evangelist as your helper..?"'[33] Evidently Fullerton and Manton Smith continued to feel undervalued. Spurgeon wrote to Fullerton in 1883: 'I have never had the most distant idea of your ever having been snubbed or tolerated. It may be so, but I have never heard a living soul at the Tabernacle speak of you except with the greatest esteem.'[34] Fullerton, Manton Smith and other College evangelists continued their ministry. In 1893, however, Fullerton was invited to become pastor of Melbourne Hall, Leicester, a church which had been started by F.B. Meyer and which had a congregation of 1,500. The College Trustees offered him £100 per year extra to continue as an evangelist but he decided to settle into a pastorate.[35] Later Fullerton was to exercise a wider ministry as Home Secretary of the BMS.

In fact, the College did not make a sharp distinction between the calling of evangelist and pastor. All pastors had to be evangelists and all evangelists had to expound scripture. Speaking at the College in 1888, Spurgeon spoke about training 'attractive' preachers and 'impressive' expositors. He praised the work of Fullerton, Manton Smith and other evangelists trained at the College, and also commended the Salvation Army for going to 'the masses'. Spurgeon warned trainee preachers to avoid complacency. He did not want the people 'to go to sleep under your ministry', or leave because it was so dull, but he wanted people to 'throng to hear it'.[36] When Robert Hughes, a member of the Metropolitan Tabernacle who attended the church's training class in connection with its Society of Evangelists, wanted to enter the College, Spurgeon felt he needed more experience in mission. Spurgeon suggested to Hughes that he undertake evangelistic outreach in Wales. This was not what Hughes wanted to hear, but an elder at the Tabernacle advised him: 'If the Pastor wants you to go to South Wales, you had better go and he will be your friend. But if you refuse he will drop you, and may never take you up again.' Hughes moved to South Wales, where his evangelistic work was successful and where he became involved in founding and leading a new church. Spurgeon then invited him to enter the College. At the end of his College training Hughes had approaches from churches in England, but was not sure about his future until Spurgeon once more intervened and said: 'Make a trip to America'. Hughes left in 1888 and had a long and distinguished ministry in Ohio.[37] Effective evangelists were often significant pastors.

Changing methods in mission

With the death of C.H. Spurgeon it became more difficult to sustain aspects of the evangelistic work which he had supported. His brother, James Spurgeon, who took over in 1892 as President of the College, spoke in the 1892-93 College report of the money expended in Home Mission work, in 'aiding the preaching-stations originated by the late President', and also mentioned that he had 'made it a rule to redeem every promise made by the late Pastor...towards any extension of work now being carried on'.[38] This proved, however, to be impossible. When W.Y. Fullerton left his work with the College Society of Evangelists to enter pastoral ministry the question of on-going financial support for Manton Smith proved to be highly problematic. The Trustees of the College suggested in 1895 (by which time only Manton Smith and John Burnham remained as College Society evangelists) that Manton Smith might be transferred to a team that had been created - referred to as 'Mrs Spurgeon's staff of evangelists'. Probably there was a hope that evangelists operating under Susannah Spurgeon's name had a better chance of attracting financial backers. Mrs Spurgeon, however, indicated that she could not help Manton Smith.[39] By the twentieth century the financial support of the Society of Evangelists by the College proved to be untenable.

New initiatives, however, were apparent. Two brothers, E.A. Carter and F.C. Carter, who trained at the College, became involved in church planting in the 1880s. E.A. Carter developed a wider itinerant ministry and in 1889 founded the Pioneer Mission. The aims were to increase weak Baptist churches, to commence new Baptist causes and to evangelise generally. Initially there was a focus on the North-West of England, but the work spread.[40] E.A. Carter, in the College's 1895-96 report, spoke enthusiastically of the Pioneer Mission starting churches in Scotland. The Gourock church was 'steadily growing in numbers and influence' and its leader, Lachlan McPhail, had entered the Pastors' College. Similar activity was taking place across England. At Pinchbeck, in Lincolnshire, where Baptists were 'almost extinct', a new chapel had been built and the Pioneer Mission was helping to resuscitate the work. There was no Nonconformist minister in this parish of 8,000 people. The Baptist church in East Molesey, Hampton Court, was in 'a very low state', and two local ministers, said Carter, 'asked us to take charge'. A six-week mission was organised. Carter was delighted that in 'almost all our places' there was advance, and that several local Pioneer Mission leaders had been accepted to study at the College.[41] Whereas earlier the College had been the spring-board for mission, by the end of the nineteenth century it was benefitting from the fruit of enterprising leaders such as Carter. Later, in 1920, Caradoc Jones, who had trained at the College, began work in Brittany with the Pioneer Mission. This led to the founding of a church and an orphanage. During the Second World War Jones spent four years in a concentration camp, and gave himself to demanding ministry there.[42]

The early twentieth century also saw advance through revival. Baptists were deeply affected by the Welsh Revival of 1904-5, a huge people movement which came in part out of a desire felt by some young Welsh ministers for personal revival. One of them, Owen Owen, who trained at the College in the 1890s, received help at a Convention for the deepening of spiritual life in Llandrindod Wells in 1903.[43] Archibald McCaig showed great interest in the leading figure in the Welsh Revival, a young former miner, Evan Roberts. In January 1905 McCaig visited Wales and reported on what he called God's 'wonderful

*Welsh Students 1905. Standing left to right:
Austin Edwards, Caradoc Jones,
J.R. Edwards, D.E. Davies,
Seated left to right: Thomas Hayward,
Frank Williams*

works', and in particular on the powerful preaching of Roberts.[44] McCaig made a return visit to Wales with Thomas Spurgeon, who was also deeply impressed. Owen Owen acted as their interpreter since most of the services were in Welsh. Thomas Spurgeon began special prayer meetings at the Tabernacle in March 1905 at which six College students from Wales were prominent. All of them had been affected by the Revival during the Christmas vacation and Caradoc Jones reported on nearly 800 people converted in his home area through the preaching of a Baptist minister, R.B. Jones.[45] The prayer meetings at the Metropolitan Tabernacle were followed by a mission in the Elephant and Castle area conducted by College staff and students, led by the six Welsh students, and 745 professions of conversion were made.[46] McCaig was fully engaged in open-air meetings – in his top hat and frock coat - and later emphasised that this experience in the life of the College was not a passing revivalist phenomenon.[47]

There was also increasing emphasis in the period before the Second World War on team-work in evangelistic campaigns.[48] In the 1930s five ministers came together in Essex to form an evangelistic team under the leadership of Hugh McCullough, pastor of Dagenham Baptist Church, who had trained at Spurgeon's in the early 1920s. Another member of the team, Fred G. Missen from Burnham-on-Crouch, had also trained at the College. The ministers were released by their churches to spend a week each month in wider evangelism. They came to be known as the 'Essex Five'. Stanley Baker, of Tabernacle Baptist Church, Grays, the team secretary, had been brought into ministry through Douglas Brown (the son of Archibald Brown), who led a revival in East Anglia in the early 1920s.[49] In 1934, Hugh McCulloch reporting on what was being experienced in Essex Baptist churches through the team, spoke of some experiences as 'nothing less than revival', with 30-40 people coming to enquiry rooms at the end of meetings.[50] Other mission teams were led by College students, and summer campaigns continued into the War years. In 1941, for example, William Goodwin reported on a typical campaign in Dudley, in the Midlands, entitled 'Crusade for Christ', which saw decisions for Christ at all the evening meetings. Goodwin remarked that he found returning to Greek verbs and Hebrew paradigms difficult after his experiences in the Crusade.[51]

Evangelistic endeavours

Immediately after the War, there was evidence of a new evangelistic thrust in Britain. An American Youth for Christ team arrived in Britain in March 1946. Billy Graham was one of its members and he was to become the leading evangelist of the twentieth century. This forty-six day visit, which involved many evangelistic events, followed by six months of mission which Graham conducted throughout Britain from October 1946, brought fresh vision in many places, and the contacts that Graham made led to the massive Harringay Crusade in London during the first three months of 1954. College students went to a seminar on evangelism during the last week of the Crusade.[52] George Beasley-Murray later spoke of the number of students who came to Spurgeon's who had either been converted or called to ministry through Billy Graham meetings.[53] When, in 1964, *The Christian* ran a series of testimonies from Harringay converts, the person featured who had entered pastoral ministry was Peter Pearmain, who trained at Spurgeon's.[54] Another development was the growth of the Inter-Varsity Fellowship, which drew together Christian Unions in the universities. In November 1947 Spurgeon's students were involved in the organisation and leadership of a London Inter-Faculty Christian Union (LIFCU) mission designed to reach the thousands of students in London. Nearly 170 meetings were held including five united meetings at King's College London with average attendances of 500-600 students.[55] In a number of the post-war College campaigns there was an emphasis on reaching teenagers. At Hoddesdon Baptist Church, in September 1946, nine teenagers 'made the great decision for Christ' and others were 'stirred to a greater zeal for Christ'.[56]

Summer campaigns continued, and in 1954 Raymond Brown, then a student, reported on encouraging results in Worthing (Broadwater), Croydon (New Addington), South Norwood, Horsham (Trafalgar Road), Thornton Heath, and Birmingham (Harborne).[57] More campaigns were planned. Two years later, however, the College students reported that although they had brought vitality to the churches through their missions they had largely failed to reach and confront non-churchgoers with the claims of Christ. They had found themselves, said Alan Griggs and Leslie Jell, preaching evangelistic sermons to church members. This influenced seven College students to become involved with the Luton Industrial Mission under the leadership of William Gowland. The Industrial Mission aimed not only to win people for Christ but to redeem society. Gradually the emphasis on social action – an emphasis which characterised Spurgeon's own ministry – would become prominent in local mission undertaken by ministers trained at the College. The Spurgeon's students in Luton were part of a team of fifty theological college students. Spurgeon's students felt they had seen the church in action in a new and dynamic way.[58] Another new development for the College was the use of skiffle music in evangelism. A music group was formed by Bryan Gilbert, a student with a background in music, to engage in evangelism directed towards young people. This was discussed by the College Council in April 1958. It was reported that the students supported the new initiative but the faculty 'had expressed its strong distaste for the use of this kind of music with Gospel songs'. The Council, which was divided on the issue, agreed not to ban the skiffle group, but to say to the students that the College should not be identified with it.[59]

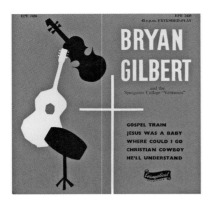

Two records by The Venturers

George Beasley-Murray, the new Principal, was keen to encourage evangelism and was supportive of what Bryan Gilbert and his group were seeking to do.[60] In the summer of 1958 a team from the College formed a 'South Coast Venture Team' for a mission in Brighton, with the music group participating. A year later the group, which became known as the Venturers, was involved in evangelism in coffee bars in Liverpool.[61] In autumn 1963, a mission to Dagenham involved the four Dagenham Baptist churches. The Dagenham group was an early experiment in team ministry sponsored by the Baptist Union and the Essex Baptist Association. The mission included large youth meetings, a coffee bar, talks in schools and factories, and a Saturday morning cinema club which attracted many children. Over fifty students and staff took part, working with the three ministers – J.J. Brown, W.H. Campbell and Roy Cave – all of whom had trained at the College, and a Deaconess, Sister Margaret.[62] The Venturers proved to be an important training ground for evangelistic work, and continued under the leadership of Michael Wood. Records were produced. A number of those involved in the group committed themselves to working together in Baptist ministry in Rochdale. Among other initiatives in the 1960s, students participated in 1967 in a 'Church and Society' course in connection with the West Ham Central Mission, under the leadership of Colin Marchant, who studied at Spurgeon's in the early 1950s. Colin Marchant later introduced many College students to issues in urban ministry. Since many College students were from middle-class suburban or small town churches gaining insights into inner city ministry was of crucial importance.[63]

During the 1960s George Beasley-Murray gave evangelism a high profile and this evangelistic emphasis was continued by Raymond Brown. In 1967 Beasley-Murray said that when he was asked to summarise the aim of the College, his answer was: 'To produce pastor-evangelists who can build up the churches.' The answer, he added, was framed with the example in mind of Spurgeon, who was the pastor-evangelist *par excellence*. In expanding on his thinking, Beasley-Murray suggested that pastors needed to preach the whole gospel, which meant grappling with the whole Bible and with the Holy Spirit's illumination in the Church though the ages. 'To achieve that on a significant scale', he considered, 'is an immense task. It is complicated by the fact that men and women today are out of touch with the message of the Gospel. Their thought is moulded by agencies which take no account of God, and therefore which, for practical purposes, are atheistic.'[64] As examples of how these themes were developed by students from this period, David Beer, at Frinton Free Church, explored and wrote about ways of undertaking mission through the local church, and Philip Clements-Jewery, in addition to his pastorates, became Director of the ecumenical Christian Enquiry Agency. Beasley-Murray hoped for financial help from the Billy Graham Evangelistic Association for a College lecturership in Evangelism. Although this was not forthcoming, support from the First Baptist Church of Memphis, USA, and the Foreign Mission Board of the Southern Baptist Convention, enabled Lewis Drummond to be appointed as lecturer in Evangelism and Pastoral Instruction. Drummond had studied at Southwestern Baptist Seminary, Texas, had held pastorates in the USA, and had a PhD from King's College London.[65]

Church growth and church planting

When Raymond Brown became Principal in 1973 he soon engaged with wider Baptist thinking about the future of the ministry. A report entitled *Ministry Tomorrow* (1969) foresaw a marked decline in full-time Baptist ministers, but Brown noted in 1974 that recent discussion in the Baptist Union Council suggested that the Union was short of ministers.[66] In response to the publication by the Baptist Union in 1980 of *A Call to Commitment – Baptist Christians through the 1980s*, in which the Baptist Union General Secretary, David Russell, encouraged discussion of aspects of commitment, Raymond Brown wrote articles about the contribution made by the College to these areas, highlighting in 1982 the theme of commitment to evangelism. College missions, spearheaded by Peter Manson, were continuing, former students were engaging in mission overseas, and in Britain ministers trained at Spurgeon's were engaged in church-based evangelism. Stephen Ibbotson, who trained in the 1970s, engaged in significant Baptist church planting in Peterborough. The College *Record* featured in 1974 work being done by Bryan Gilbert, with 'One Step Forward' (OSF), and by Vic Jackopson, with 'Evangelism Explosion' or 'Teach and Reach' (T & R). Graham Allen, who after training at the College began ministry at Mill End, Rickmansworth, said that OSF material had been the primary reason behind the recent growth in his church. Paul Beasley-Murray, then senior minister at Altrincham Baptist Church, estimated from research he had undertaken that Baptist churches using T & R had grown by an average of 23%.[67]

The research being done by Paul Beasley-Murray was indicative of a new interest in the 1980s in church growth. Paul Beasley-Murray's study was entitled *Turning the Tide*, and as well as analysing churches it developed a model of growth.[68] When Beasley-Murray was

Steve Chalke

appointed Principal in 1986 he was committed to church planting and church growth, and to introducing courses which offered training in these areas. Under the banner of SALT – Spurgeon's Adaptable Leadership Training – he encouraged the growth of part-time as well as full-time training. The College Council had noted in 1984 that Regent's Park College, Oxford, and Northern College, Manchester, had alternative methods of training.[69] In 1988 there was a high intake of full-time students at Spurgeon's: fifteen of those entering were taking a college-based course (the traditional mode of training) whereas seventeen were taking a church-based course. This represented significant growth in the student intake and also indicated the way training was changing. In the same year it was agreed that the College would start an Evangelism and Church Planting course, in partnership with Oasis Trust, a rapidly-growing agency for evangelism and social concern founded by Steve Chalke, a Spurgeon's student in the later 1970s. A particular emphasis on urban mission developed. Research showed that of the Spurgeon's students who had settled in the home ministry from the mid-1970s to the mid-1980s one-third had settled in inner-city situations.[70] Stuart Christine, who trained at Spurgeon's in the 1970s and served with the BMS in Brazil (where he had considerable experience in theological education), became a New Testament tutor at the College and then the first Oasis Director of Church Planting and Evangelism. College growth continued, with fifty students commencing church-based, mission-based and college-based courses in 1989. The total full-time student body reached 130. There was a significant emphasis, under Paul Beasley-Murray, on the College producing theologically trained evangelists.

The concern for urban and also cross-cultural mission led to a number of new developments. A course was started on Asian thought and practice, led by Ram Gidoomal, Director of South Asian Concern, and by Stuart Murray, who succeeded Stuart Christine in 1992 as director of the Church Planting and Evangelism course. Bill Allen, who joined the College staff at the same time, forged strong links with a variety of departments within the Borough of Croydon, and this formed another aspect of student exposure to urban realities. A major initiative, initially in East London, was Urban Expression, launched in 1997 in partnership with the College and Oasis Trust. Stuart Murray, who had been involved in church planting in Tower Hamlets, saw Urban Expression as a vehicle for inner-city ministry. Colin Marchant was also an important facilitator in this area. Juliet Kilpin, who entered Baptist ministry in 1996 having trained at Spurgeon's, became part-time co-ordinator of

Urban Expression and an associate lecturer at Spurgeon's. She and her husband, Jim, also a Baptist minister trained at Spurgeon's, led the first Urban Expression church planting team. By the end of 2004 there were seven Urban Expression church planting teams in London and further expansion to other parts of the country was envisaged.[71] Several teams were led by former Spurgeon's students. The College's innovative forms of training meant that students who were not seeking accredited Baptist ministry came to the College to train. In 1994, for example, seventeen of the forty-four new full-time students were not at that stage intending to enter Baptist Union accredited ministry, although some transferred during their course.

Juliet and Jim Kilpin

From October 2002 a further new course in evangelism was introduced. This was intended to train those who would become 'competent and effective advocates of the Christian message in a wide variety of settings'. Like the Church Planting and Evangelism course, this new pathway was developed in conjunction with Oasis. Although there was an intention to attract students from different denominations and organisations, the course was designed to be a recognised means of training towards accreditation as an evangelist with the Baptist Union. The College was convinced of the need to prepare a generation of

Playground project undertaken by Urban Expression

evangelists to speak for Christ in a society in which Christianity had been substantially displaced. It was anticipated that trained evangelists might in the future function as full-time, part-time or voluntary workers or might be 'bi-vocational', seeing their present employment as part of their ministry. In the light of this the modes of training offered were flexible. The communities to be reached by these evangelists were increasingly diverse, and it was considered important that evangelists trained by Spurgeon's should come from diverse and varied contexts. In the view of the College – and here there was an echo of W.Y. Fullerton's thinking - it was important not to operate with a 'stereotype' of what an evangelist was, but rather to seek creative diversity - men and women, black and white, traditional and non-traditional, young and old.[72] Rachel Dutton, who was appointed course

Rachel Dutton

leader in 2002, had been on the staff of St Andrew's Church, Chorleywood, responsible for evangelism and discipleship.

Conclusion

From its beginning the College gave high priority to training students to be effective in evangelism, whether as pastors or as those in full-time evangelistic ministry. John W. Ewing, who trained at the College in the 1880s and had a significant ministry at Rye Lane Chapel, Peckham (which became one of the largest churches in south London), until during the First World War he became the Metropolitan Area Superintendent and Secretary of the London Baptist Association, spoke in 1906 of what he had received from his training at the College. He had gained, he said, 'a sense of the value of the cross', 'an impulse towards soul-winning', especially the need 'to speak face to face with my hearers, bringing every power I possess to bear upon the work of leading men and women to Christ', and 'the supremacy of the spiritual'.[73] The emphasis given to effective evangelism was evident. George Beasley-Murray made it clear sixty years later that he had no interest in the College producing evangelists who were 'slick salesmen of religion'. He wanted proper academic disciplines, and argued that College students had never been better grounded in the Bible and aware of the need to communicate in ways that people could understand.[74] Equipping evangelists has remained important. Dennis Pethers, trained in the 1980s, worked with the Sussex Association and later pioneered the Viz-A-Viz evangelistic agency. With the launch of the new course to train evangelists it was stressed that evangelists needed to be deeply rooted in the scriptures and in the Christian way of believing and living, so that they could advocate the gospel with intelligence and understanding, and also that they needed to understand contemporary culture.[75] The College was aiming to help those who would, in line with C.H. Spurgeon's vision that a truly prophetic ministry was always evangelistic, be skilled at bringing people to personal faith and discipleship and who would also be able to apply the Christian message to the contemporary world.

1   *S and T*, April 1870, p. 10.

2   Spurgeon, *Autobiography*, Vol. 2, pp. 146-7.

3   Carlile, *C.H. Spurgeon: An Interpretative Biography*, p. 170. E.W. Bacon, in *Spurgeon: Heir of the Puritans* (London: George Allen & Unwin, 1967), p. 91, makes an unfortunate error in saying that Thomas Medhurst became the head of a strange sect in America. Bacon is confusing Thomas Medhurst with C.S. Medhurst, his son – see chapter 5 below.

4   *AP*, 1884-85, p. 3.

5   C.H. Spurgeon, 'A word of thankfulness from the President', *Outline*, 1868, p. 3.

6   *S and T*, June 1881, p. 305.

7   *AP*, 1891-92, p. 12; M. Nicholls, *C.H. Spurgeon: The Pastor Evangelist* (Didcot: Baptist Historical Society), p. 99.

8   *S and T*, January 1866, p. 43.

9   *S and T*, May 1866, pp. 227-9.

10 *S and T*, November 1867, p. 500.

11 *S and T*, April 1873, p. 147.

12 I.S. Drummond, 'The Spurgeon Legacy', CNAA BA Dissertation (1990), p. 44. This is a detailed analysis of the church planting strategy and achievements of Spurgeon.

13 Nicholls, *C.H. Spurgeon: The Pastor Evangelist*, pp. 98-9.

14 *Outline*, 1867, p. 69.

15 *S and T*, March 1865, p. 130.

16 *Outline*, 1868, p. 21; *East London Tabernacle* (London: East London Tabernacle, 1956).

17 *S and T*, March 1867, p. 132.

18 *S and T*, April 1867, p. 187.

19 *S and T*, September 1867, p. 431.

20 H. Moncrieff, *Roots of Labour* (Yeovil: Linden Hall, 1990), pp. 54-60.

21 *S and T*, March 1869, p. 141.

22 *S and T*, April 1873, p. 147.

23 *S and T*, May 1882, p. 260.

24 Fullerton, *Spurgeon*, pp. 239-40. For the songs used see *Evangelical Echoes and Song Services* (London: Passmore and Alabaster, n.d.) - held in the College Heritage Room.

25 *S and T*, June 1881, p. 305.

26 G.W. Harte, *Historical Tablets* (Southport: Thomas Seddon, 1951), p.39.

27 *S and T*, June 1884, p. 294.

28 R. Shindler, *From the Usher's Desk to the Tabernacle Pulpit* (London: Passmore and Alabaster, 1892), pp. 154-7.

29 Minutes of the Regent's Park Chapel Church Meeting held on 26 January 1891: I.M. Randall, *Spirituality and Social Change* (Carlisle: Paternoster Press, 2003), pp. 119-20.

30 Shindler, *From the Usher's Desk*, pp. 142-3.

31 Ibid., p. 155.

32 *S and T*, January 1881, p. 19.

33 Ibid, p. 20

34 C.H. Spurgeon to W.Y. Fullerton, 1 October 1883 - held in Heritage Room

35 Minutes of Pastors' College Trustees, 2 November 1893; Trustees of Pastors' College to W.Y. Fullerton, 3

November 1893; Fullerton to Trustees, 11 November 1893; Fullerton to Trustees, 25 November 1893 (College Minute Book, 1893-98, Box 14).

36 *S and T*, November 1888, pp. 569-74.

37 *College Record*, April 1949, pp. 12-17.

38 *AP*, 1892-93, p. 4.

39 Minutes of Meetings of Pastors' College Trustees, 13 June 1895, 11 July 1895,

40 Shindler, *From the Usher's Desk*, pp. 162-3; Harte, *Historical Tablets*, p. 51; Nicholls, *C.H. Spurgeon: The Pastor Evangelist*, pp. 108-9.

41 *AP*, 1895-96, pp. 46-7.

42 *College Record*, December 1950, pp. 22-3; W.M. Pearce, *Knight in Royal Service* (London: Pioneer Mission, 1962).

43 B.P. Jones, *The King's Champions* (Cwmbran, Gwent: Christian Literature Press, 1968), p. 48; E. Evans, *The Welsh Revival of 1904* (London: Evangelical Press, 1969).

44 *S and T*, February 1905, pp. 66-70.

45 *S and T*, February 1905, p. 66; March 1905, pp. 122-9, 145-6; April 1905, pp. 179-81.

46 *S and T*, May 1905, pp. 220-7, 239.

47 *S and T*, June 1906, pp. 278-9.

48 See REKABAS, *An Adventure for God* (London: Kingsgate Press, 1934); Doris Witard, *Bibles in Barrels: A History of Essex Baptists* (Southend-on-Sea: Essex Baptist Association, 1962), chapter 22.

49 For this revival, see S.C. Griffin, *Forgotten Revival* (Bromley: Day One Publications, 1992).

50 Minutes of the Baptist Union Discipleship Campaign, 25 January 1934.

51 *Spurgeon's College Magazine*, Christmas 1941, pp. 12-13.

52 I.M. Randall, 'Conservative Constructionist: The Early Influence of Billy Graham in Britain', *The Evangelical Quarterly*, Vol. 67, No. 4 (1995), pp. 309-33.

53 P. Beasley-Murray, *Fearless for Truth: A Personal Portrait of the Life of George Beasley-Murray* (Carlisle: Paternoster Press, 2002), p. 76.

54 *The Christian*, 29 May 1964, p. 4.

55 *Spurgeon's College Magazine*, Autumn 1947, p. 25.

56 *Spurgeon's College Magazine*, Autumn 1946, p. 21.

57 *College Record*, May 1955, pp. 29-30.

58 *College Record*, July 1957, pp. 2-6.

59 Minutes of College Council, 14 April 1958.

60 Beasley-Murray, *Fearless for Truth*, pp. 102-3.

61 *Baptist Times*, [hereafter BT] 14 August 1958, p. 12; 28 May 1959, p. 4.

62 *College Record*, December 1963, pp. 17-19; BT, 17 October 1963, p. 2.

63 *College Record*, June 1967, pp. 3-5.

64 *College Record*, December 1967, pp. 2-4.

65 Executive Committee Minutes, 29 September 1967; *College Record*, December 1968, pp. 4-5.

66 *College Record*, June 1974, p. 4.

67 *College Record*, December 1982, pp. 15-17; cf. *A Call to Commitment – Baptist Christians through the 1980s* (London: Baptist Union, 1980).

68 P. Beasley-Murray and A. Wilkinson, *Turning the Tide* (London: The Bible Society, 1981).

69 Minutes of College Council, 10 and 11 April 1984.

70 A Thompson, 'Ministerial Training from a London Perspective', 20 May 1985, with Executive Committee Minutes of 19 June; Minutes of Ministerial Training Working Group on 22 May 1985.

71 From the Urban Expression website, http://www.urbanexpression.org.uk

72 *Training at Spurgeon's College: Evangelists' Course*, 2004, pp. 2-5.

73 *S and T*, June 1906, pp. 286-7.

74 *College Record*, December 1967, pp. 2-4.

75 *Training at Spurgeon's College: Evangelists' Course*, pp. 2-3.

Chapter 4: Shaping spiritual leaders

In 1870 C.H. Spurgeon said regarding the role of the College: 'It appears to us that the maintenance of a truly spiritual College is probably the readiest way in which to bless the churches.'[1] The emphasis on 'a truly spiritual College' was central to Spurgeon's concept of ministerial training. It was not that the College could in itself produce spirituality. Rather the proper spiritual commitment that was essential for ministry had already to be evident. Those being trained, Spurgeon insisted, must be 'full of the Holy Ghost, called of God to their work, anointed, qualified, and divinely sustained'.[2] One key task of the College was to nurture the spiritual life of each student. A 'school of the prophets' was a school of spiritual development. During the first half of its life, when the College was non-residential and was associated with the Metropolitan Tabernacle, an important part of the way in which students were developed spiritually was through their participation in church life. From 1923, with the change to a residential College, the emphasis was much more on the ways by which the spiritual well-being of the community could be fostered. With the more recent development of church-based training courses, which in the 1990s became the most common pathway into ordained ministry, there has been a move back to the concept of the local church as a significant context for spiritual growth.

An earthy spirituality

A crucial element in Spurgeon's thinking about spiritual development was the belief that healthy spirituality flourished when people were in touch with ordinary life rather than being detached from it. His vision was of an earthy spirituality. This was clearly set out by Spurgeon in *The Sword and the Trowel* in 1870 when he spoke about the life of the students at the College:

> The young brethren are boarded generally in twos and threes, in the houses of our friends around the Tabernacle, for which the College pays a moderate weekly amount…The plan of separate lodging we believe to be far preferable to having all under one roof, for by the latter mode men are isolated from general family habits…The circumstances of the families who entertain our young friends are generally such that they are not elevated above the social position which in all probability they will have to occupy in future years.[3]

In addition to living in the homes of the people who attended the Tabernacle, students also visited homes in their neighbourhoods to distribute copies of Spurgeon's sermons. They met a great deal of indifference as they tried to engage people in conversation. At the same time, there were a good number of people who came to the Tabernacle as a result of the visiting. In one year over 2,000 homes were visited. The benefit of being in touch with the problems of the localities around the Tabernacle was emphasised. Over time these arrangements altered. By the end of the nineteenth century many of the students were no longer in the homes of local people. Some were boarded out as far as Blackheath and were often in large houses. One house, for example, accommodated fourteen students. But the principle of connecting with day-to-day living was still regarded as important.[4]

The link between the College and the Tabernacle's worshipping life was also intentional. Involvement in church activities kept students in touch with the realities of ministry. The church members were encouraged to talk to and encourage students and this kind of conversation, said George Rogers in 1866, 'contributes much to their [the students] social and their spiritual welfare'. In addition, the leaders at the Tabernacle looked out for students so that they could 'cheer them by their kindness and aid them by their counsel'. For Rogers, these experiences were a vital part of training. Much of it was enjoyable, although there was also a need to learn about church discipline. He argued that lack of contact with 'a flourishing Church' was a 'serious deficiency in a College education', not least because the life of the church served to undercut ideas of hierarchy that could characterise academic institutions. Within the church and College community, Rogers noted, personal friendships were valued. 'No deference is required by any', he commented, 'that is not spontaneously given.'[5] Two decades on, with experience of how the College and the church related to each other, Rogers still held the same views. In the College report for 1883-84 he reflected on how the College's connection with 'a pastorate of great order, extent, and vitality' had produced results that had 'exceeded the most sanguine expectations'. The real work in ministry, he contended, was being done by those who prized spirituality – depending 'less upon the wisdom of man and more upon the power of God.'[6] Church life reinforced this priority.

Although Spurgeon shared Rogers' views about College training, he was realistic about the pressures former students faced in ministry and the need for a robust on-going spirituality. Speaking to former and current students at the College Conference meetings in 1880, in an address entitled 'A New Departure', he warned about the danger of routine. Spurgeon noted that 'we are very apt to run down through *our duty becoming routine work*, by reason of its monotony. Unless we are careful, we shall be likely to say to ourselves, "Monday evening here again, I must give an address at the prayer-meeting. Thursday evening, and I have to preach, although I have not yet a topic! Sunday morning, Sunday evening…What a weariness it is!"' In the light of this Spurgeon advocated openness to 'the daily anointing of the Spirit', but also – again he was realistic - meeting with others 'of warm heart and of kindred spirit'. He suggested signs which sometimes indicated a loss of spiritual energy, for example an absorption with hobbies or an obsession with prophecy - in the sense of predictions about the future. Some preachers, Spurgeon said, 'having lost their love of the gospel, try to win back what little popularity they once had by taking up with guesses at the future'.[7] As he often did, Spurgeon issued a challenge to more adventurous spiritual living. 'We are come', he pronounced later in his address, 'to the kingdom for such a time as this.' Using the examples of the Dutch Anabaptist leader, Menno Simons, and seventeenth-century English Baptist figures - Hanserd Knollys, William Kiffin and Benjamin Keach – he urged students and ministers to be 'bold to stand the brunt of the battle for the Lord'.[8]

Such a statement typifies the concern for the individual in Spurgeon's approach to spirituality. The College courses that students undertook were often tailored to their individual needs. There was a desire to develop each trainee in such a way as to ensure the best result possible. In 1881 Spurgeon reported that over the year there had been 120 students in College. Two years was normal but this was lengthened to three years. The significant point was that an assessment was made of each student. In some cases further training was judged counter-productive since 'to detain them from their work is to repress their ardour without bestowing a compensatory advantage'. In other cases, Spurgeon argued, a longer period in College was better, so that students went out 'more thoroughly prepared'. Some churches called students away before the end of the course. When students were kept longer at College, Spurgeon recalled, 'the good deacons of the eager churches thought me a sort of a harsh jailer, who locked up his prisoners'.[9] In the first half of the twentieth century the format of training became more uniform, but from the 1970s more flexibility was again evident. College interview procedures highlighted concern for the individual. Church-based training and an emphasis on supervised placements for all students had a significant impact. Bob Archer, who trained at the College in the 1950s and had ministries in Bournemouth, Canterbury, Worcester Park and Reading, before becoming a tutor in 1990, gave great energy to church-based pastoral training, including the supervision of placements. Later John Murray, a College student in the 1960s who had ministries in Blackheath and Eastbourne, was a chaplain in HM Forces, and was Secretary to the United Navy, Army and Air Force Board, assisted part-time. From 2001 a full-time member of staff, Linda Smith, co-ordinated all placements. Spurgeon's has engaged seriously with the vision for practical formation.

Spirituality and scholarship

It was a regular complaint in Spurgeonic circles that there was too much stress on scholarship in the training offered for the ministry in other colleges. 'Collegiate training', George Rogers noted in 1866, 'had hitherto been limited to a particular class of candidates, and to a particular kind and amount of education…The literary attainments of our ministers, it has been said, must advance with the literature of the age.' Rogers asked if students trained by these methods were known to have more impact as ministers and he answered with a resounding 'No!' It was against this background that the College had been formed and had developed as a 'new method of collegiate training, better adapted to the real wants of the age'.[10] What the College aimed at was not to reach people of 'high culture' but to be relevant to the needs of the majority of the population, and reaching the 'common people' could not be achieved, as Spurgeon put it, by preachers who 'affect obscurity, quote Strauss, frequently speak of Goethe (careful as to the pronunciation of his name)' and in fact know a little of everything 'except vital godliness and Puritanic divinity'.[11] One of Spurgeon's objects of contempt was 'modern thought'. Speaking to the

Charles Spurgeon
(son of C.H. Spurgeon)

Pastors' Conference in 1874, he stated: 'Our "modern thought" gentry are doing incalculable mischief to the souls of men. ....Highly cultured soul-murderers will find their boasted "culture" to be no excuse in the day of judgment.'[12]

Yet the College did not see scholarship and spirituality as in complete conflict. In his expository work Spurgeon made use of rather obscure Latin authors. Indeed in 1870 Spurgeon, with the overstatement to which he was prone, lamented the 'unlettered condition' of many people in England and blamed the poor English educational system, which was, he considered, far behind that in Scotland.[13] W.Y. Fullerton, describing the Friday afternoons that Spurgeon spent with the College students, recalled that on occasions Spurgeon would read from John Milton, William Cowper, William Wordsworth and Samuel Taylor Coleridge.[14] Like the Romantic poets, Spurgeon valued the natural world, telling his students at one lecture: 'He who forgets the humming of the bees among the heather, the cooing of the wood-pigeons in the forest, the song of birds in the woods, the rippling of rills among the rushes, and the sighing of the wind among the pines, need not wonder if his heart forgets to sing and his soul grows heavy.'[15] Without any feeling of contradiction, Spurgeon also often quoted at his Friday lectures from Puritan writers. For the students the reading or the lecture 'was in itself a lesson in elocution'. Fullerton drew attention to Spurgeon's *Lectures to My Students*, which contained famous lectures such as those on 'Posture, Action and Gesture'. One critic 'of wide experience and sound judgment', said Fullerton, considered the lecture on 'The Holy Spirit in Connection with Our Ministry' the finest thing he had ever read on the Spirit's work.[16] The College combined scholarly and spiritual insights.

During the principalships of David Gracey and Archibald McCaig similar themes were reiterated. The students appreciated Gracey's lectures in Divinity, his 'lucid and devout exposition of Scripture', and work done with them in homiletics. They also knew that Gracey was interested in art, and at the celebration of twenty-one years of Gracey's work

*College Faculty c.1901
with Thomas and Charles Spurgeon
Left to right: Walter Hackney, Thomas
Spurgeon,Archibald McCaig (Principal),
Charles Spurgeon, William Gaussen*

as a tutor they presented him with two engravings of pictures by Gustave Doré, who illustrated Dante's *Inferno*.[17] Early in McCaig's principalship, C.H. Spurgeon's son Charles, as Vice-President of the College, spoke about 'a high tone of spirituality' in the College, contrasting that with the experience by which 'gain in mental culture often means loss in soul growth'. McCaig himself added that the priority of the College was not to produce students who could compose 'finished literary essays', but to produce 'Scriptural, Evangelical, Soul-winning preachers' who had 'spiritual force'.[18] McCaig was assisted in the tutorial work of the College by W.H. Gaussen, an Irishman who had an MA and LLB from Trinity College, Dublin, and Walter Hackney, who trained at the College in the 1870s and had an MA from Oxford University. In 1906 McCaig stated that the position regarding the teaching in the College was still as Spurgeon set it out, in that 'while not despising scholarship, but giving all possible attention thereto, [the College] desires to give the first place to spiritual fervour and preaching power.'[19] There was no desire on the part of either Gracey or McCaig to deviate from this position.

As a student at the College, Percy Evans had applauded the kind of teaching which avoided narrow approaches.[20] During the 1920s and early 1930s, when on the College staff, he had to contend with Fundamentalist thinking within the Baptist denomination. In 1924 Evans was invited by T.R. Glover - a liberal evangelical classical scholar who was Public Orator of Cambridge University and who was President of the Baptist Union that year - to speak at the Union Assembly. Evans agreed and hoped (against the background of attacks on Glover) his participation would be 'a symbol of unity'.[21] In 1930 a probationer Baptist minister, W.E. Dalling, resigned from the Union, launching a bitter attack in the *Baptist Times* on 'Modernist propaganda' in Baptist colleges. A magazine entitled the *Fundamentalist* sought to put pressure on Evans to separate from the 'soul-destroying errors rampant within the Baptist Union' and one anonymous Baptist writer in the *Fundamentalist* asserted that the Union was almost a synonym for infidelity.[22] There was discussion at the Baptist Union Council in 1931 about books being recommended in Baptist colleges. Evans noted that *The Religious Ideas of the Old Testament*, by Wheeler Robinson, Principal of Regent's Park College (who had a particular interest in the area of spirituality), had been criticised by some, but it was a book Evans recommended at Spurgeon's.[23] As a result of Evans' emphasis on a scholarly spirituality, an emphasis strongly reinforced by George Beasley-Murray, there was much less reference within Spurgeon's College circles in the later twentieth century than in earlier periods to a conflict between spirituality and scholarship.

All-round spirituality

There was, however, much more to the spiritual
life than study. Spurgeon spoke of an 'All-round
ministry', and this was parallelled by a wish for an
all-round spirituality. A key element in the spiritual
life, for Spurgeon, was relationships. Although he
believed strongly in individual relationship with
God, he was acutely aware of the dangers of a
minister feeling alone and isolated. 'This
loneliness', he remarked in a lecture to the College
students, 'which if I mistake not is felt by many of
my brethren, is a fertile source of depression; and
our ministers' fraternal meetings, and the
cultivation of holy intercourse with kindred minds
will, with God's blessing, help us greatly to escape
the snare.'[24] Within the life of the College
Spurgeon was very keen to foster good human
relationships. David Gracey described how
students were encouraged to wrestle with
personal difficulties without being ridiculed.
'Repression and the rule of red tape', he stated,
'are avoided.' The methods of class work were
described as 'free and elastic'.[25] Communal
spiritual development was crucial. Students also
had occasional days of relaxation together. When

*Junior Common Room at the Falkland Park
mansion in 1923*

*Dining Room at the Falkland Park mansion
in 1923*

one such day was announced a student shouted: 'A day out with the Governor! Glory!' He
was known to have a Methodist background. For another student it meant 'no Latin, no
Greek, and best of all, no horrible Hebrew roots'. The day out was with members of the
Tabernacle, Mr and Mrs C.F. Allison, who had a large house, 'Town Court', with extensive
grounds, in Orpington, Kent.[26]

The relational life of the College altered after it became a residential community in 1923.
Wardens were appointed and the communal life reflected something of the atmosphere of
a boarding school. The students were single men, most in their early twenties. From the
1920s to the 1950s the average number in residence was forty, although there was an
upsurge after the Second World War and students had to be accommodated with families
from South Norwood Baptist Church. Each year group, normally ten to fifteen students,
formed a 'batch', with batch prayer meetings held twice a week, and often members of
these batches kept in touch with each other throughout their subsequent ministries.

Student group 1896-1900

Student business was conducted in the students' Common Room. A student executive was elected, and this body of senior students had the title 'Apostles'.[27] The student community began to change, however, from the 1960s. Brian Butcher, who went on to have a long ministry in Banbury, was accepted in 1964 as a married student. Eric Robbins, who had retired from banking at aged fifty-two, began a year later. He was delighted with the times spent in prayer in the College.[28] With the move, from the 1980s, to a predominantly non-residential College, and with most of the students by that time being married, Spurgeon's began to function in a very different way, but the development of strong relationships remained a feature of College life.

Within the safe community of the College, Spurgeon encouraged openness about spiritual struggles. He spoke to the students about what he called 'the minister's fainting fits', telling them that he knew 'by most painful experience what deep depression of spirit means'. Spurgeon suggested a number of things about ministry that could cause a minister depression. He referred especially to the 'horror of great darkness' he had suffered after the tragedy when he was preaching at the Surrey Gardens Music Hall in 1856 - there were shouts of 'fire' and in the stampede seven people were killed.[29] Graham Scroggie, who studied at the College in the 1890s and who by the 1930s was the leading teacher at the Keswick Convention, was similarly willing to speak about his struggles. Scroggie's most notable ministry was at Charlotte Chapel, Edinburgh, from 1916 to 1933. In the 1940s, when he was minister of the Metropolitan Tabernacle and then tutor in Biblical Exegesis at the College, Scroggie recalled 'days of despair in my first ministry in East London.' He felt in his spiritual anguish that he would pull out of ministry. 'I have no message', he agonised, 'I have no power; I have no joy, and it will kill me.' But when he was out walking in the nearby Epping Forest, Scroggie 'met with God' and became convinced that God was telling him to make a fresh resolve to put the Bible and Christ at the centre of his ministry. Scroggie spoke to the Keswick Convention and to other audiences on a number of occasions about his spiritual journey. He was grateful, he said, that he had learned many things when studying at Spurgeon's College, but he considered that he had not learned at that time how to live the Christian life fully.[30]

Although significant figures such as Spurgeon and later Scroggie stressed the importance of a spirituality that acknowledged some of the difficult aspects of ministry, there was also a less serious side to College life. The time Spurgeon spent with his students had many light-hearted elements. 'Now you will have a brief holiday', he once said before the summer vacation. 'Your chief business...will be to take things remarkably easy. And don't get courting...Come back...with your hearts and manners uncracked.'[31] Enthusiastic cricket matches, as well as games of tennis, bowls and darts, were a feature of College life.[32] It may be that under the rather dour McCaig there was less emphasis on relaxation. Perhaps significantly, McCaig noted in 1903 that 'several brethren have suffered somewhat from nervous prostration'.[33] Football became popular in the College in the early twentieth century. A report in 1936 considered that the winning of the Theological Colleges' Football Shield by Spurgeon's (which had happened three times in

Student Football Team 1926

ten years) was 'a welcome forecast of a vigorous ministry'.[34] In the early 1960s one student, Ted Sampson, was a world-class runner, holding a British and European 440 yard record. In this period the 'needle' matches in football were with London Bible College (LBC). In one notable year the Spurgeon's team defeated LBC and won the London Theological Colleges' shield. A typical Spurgeon's report spoke of a 'pilgrimage to the shrine of St Kevan' (Ernest Kevan was LBC Principal) which included a pre-resurrection 'appearance' on the football pitch of C.H. Spurgeon, who fought an apocalyptic battle.[35] The spirit of Spurgeon lived on in ways he might not have expected.

Individual and corporate disciplines

More intentional, regular spiritual disciplines have also been a feature of College life. Spurgeon encouraged students to 'know themselves'. In 1874 he commented: 'The preacher should be great in the science of the heart, the philosophy of inward experience.' Spurgeon suggested that it was good to learn from two schools of spiritual experience, one of which stressed the 'deep depravity' in the heart even of a Christian, and the other which emphasised 'the Spirit of God as a cleansing power'. Although Spurgeon warned against those who spoke as if they had become sinless, he added: 'Do not be afraid of ever growing too holy. Do not be afraid of being too full of the Holy Spirit.'[36] This exercise in self-knowledge was not intended to foster introspection but to encourage wholeness. 'What is holiness?' Spurgeon asked. 'Is it not wholeness of character? ... It is not morality, that is a cold, lifeless statue: holiness is life.'[37] Throughout the history of the College opportunities for self-assessment have often occurred in informal conversations, but appraisal systems have formalised this aspect of spiritual development. Students have been encouraged to evaluate their own personal development and the development of their gifts. This was something that Spurgeon considered vital. He referred to a preacher who was described as having 'no more gifts for the ministry than an oyster', which he felt was a slander on the oyster, since 'that worthy bivalve shows great discretion in his openings, and he also knows

Staff comments book "Like one of his own Scotch mountains: strong and imposing..."

Staff comments book "A thick crust but it is giving way..."

T.L.Johnson

when to close'.[38] Self-awareness was a vital spiritual discipline. Later, during the principalship of Paul Beasley-Murray, self-awareness groups were utilised.

Alongside self-knowledge was the informed judgment of others. Some written comments from James Spurgeon in the 1880s indicate how students were being assessed. Some comments were acerbic: 'Talks before he is ready. *Could* think if he could be trained to keep his tongue from preventing him.' Some were more hopeful: 'A thick crust, but it is giving way, and I fancy there may be something underneath.' Others were enthusiastic, and proved to be good indicators of future ministry. David J. Hiley, who was to become well known for his ministries at Broadmead Baptist Church, Bristol, and Chatsworth Way Baptist Church, West Norwood, was already impressive as a student: 'A man of great power. Much of the Welsh orator about him. A good student.' John W. Ewing showed similar promise: 'First class in every way. One of the best in every sense of the word.'[39] When there were serious questions about someone's fitness for ministry they could be dismissed, but this happened only occasionally and only if dismissal was 'the unanimous judgment of the tutors'.[40] One student in the 1870s, T.L. Johnson, who wrote a powerful account of his life in *Twenty-Eight Years a Slave*, heard about a fellow-student receiving a 'Blue Letter'. This, he discovered, meant that the student had been advised in writing to leave the College.[41] Procedures for assessment have continued, and in a small number of cases the result of the assessments means that a student is deemed not to be suitable for ministry.

There has also, however, been the opportunity for the students to comment on the lecturers. Among the early students at the College there was a stress on abstaining from alcohol. The tutors, however, were not abstainers, and in 1941 George Dann recalled discussions in the 1870s during which students challenged tutors about this.[42] Other matters could be raised by students. In 1896 a report came to the College Trustees that one of the lecturers had stated that 'he was about to deliver a lecture in accordance with the views held by the College, but which he himself did not accept'.[43] An investigation ensued. D.J. Barrow, on behalf of the students, explained that they were dissatisfied because Frederick Marchant, the acting Principal, had indicated his personal belief in universal atonement. Marchant added that his views had been known and understood by C.H. Spurgeon. Thomas Spurgeon spoke to Marchant, who insisted that in his lectures he gave students the arguments put forward by John Owen, Charles Hodge and A.A. Hodge, who taught that Christ died only for the elect ('limited atonement'), but that he did not hold that view.   It was decided by the Trustees that he should no longer deliver theological lectures. Marchant's health was not good and he later resigned as a tutor.[45] McCaig then became Principal. After the end of McCaig's principalship, the position on the atonement espoused by Marchant became more commonly held in College circles. It was rare for students to raise matters about lecturers officially, as was done with Marchant. More often, students found subtler ways of operating. In the 1930s it was known that J.F. Taviner, a tutor from 1925 to 1938, could be sidetracked from rather tedious material on philosophy to subjects of more interest to students.[46]

Finally, and crucially, there was the spiritual discipline of daily prayer and worship, which has always been central to the life of the College. Speaking in 1881 about the College's aims, Spurgeon said that the primary aim was 'the promotion of a vigorous spiritual life among those who are preparing to be under-shepherds of Christ's flock' and that 'frequent meetings for prayer' – these took place each morning and afternoon in College - were designed 'to maintain a high tone of spirituality'.[47] Six years later he talked about how students gained from participating in prayer meetings at the Metropolitan Tabernacle, adding, with amazing confidence, that 'the most varied and remarkable meetings for prayer that have been known to any age of the church, are those which are held in the Tabernacle'.[48] During Percy Evans' principalship and beyond, the pattern was that the Principal conducted worship each morning, with other prayer meetings being held during the week. G.J.M. Pearce, a student in this period, commented, however, that although 'exhortations to pray were frequent; guidance was extremely rare'.[49] When George Beasley-Murray became Principal, Geoffrey Rusling, who taught church history and who became Vice-Principal, noted the lead given by the new Principal. Rusling commented on how Beasley-Murray quickly communicated his spirit and ideals to the students.[50] In 1957 a new College Chapel was opened, built as a result of a centenary appeal - and designed by a former student, Clifford Measday, who was an architect before coming to College.

The College chapel became the venue for daily College worship and over the years has been at the heart of the life of the College community. In fact it has often been the place where some of the key aspects of training most obviously interact. It is one of the places where ministerial and spiritual formation occurs, where gifting is discovered and inter-denominational and international vision is inspired. In the 1980s it was common for the tutors to lead College chapel on most mornings but since then students and other staff members have taken a more regular role. Successive Principals have invited a variety of visitors to lead worship, preach, or lead retreats in the chapel. Different worship styles, liturgies and traditions have been explored. On occasions services from the chapel have been broadcast on radio. As well as the daily times of corporate worship, the College chapel is always open for personal prayer and reflection. During Easter 2004 the chapel was set out in such a way as to encourage meditation on the cross and the resurrection by individual students and staff. This guided meditation was entitled 'The Journey'. Many students speak of the experience of College chapel, the place of community worship, as having a lasting effect on their lives and ministries.[51]

The renewal of spirituality

At the beginning of the twentieth century the College felt the impact of the heightened spirituality of the Welsh Revival. In his report on the College in 1905, Thomas Spurgeon considered that for the students the 'memory of these meetings in which the Spirit of God was outpoured, the experience gained by visiting, enquiry room and open-air work will be a life long blessing'.[52] In similar vein McCaig wrote: 'It is usually our joy to testify to the true spirituality of the brethren, special attention being always given to the devotional side of student-life; and we are glad this year to record that the breath of Revival has been felt among us.'[53] Revival was spoken about in College circles in the 1920s when Douglas Brown, from Ramsden Road, Balham, led powerful meetings in London Road Baptist Church, Lowestoft. The 1922 College Conference included talks on 'Revival' and news from Lowestoft.[54] Concern for revival led to the Baptist Revival Fellowship (BRF) being formed in 1938.[55] Its leader, Theo Bamber, who trained at the College and was minister of the 900-member Rye Lane Chapel in Peckham from 1926, was a significant figure calling for revival. The first major BRF meeting was held in Bloomsbury Central Baptist Church in 1942. Frederick Cawley described how a 'youthful "Spurgeonic" platform drew a congregation that packed the building'. Theo Bamber and Geoffrey King, who was at College in the 1930s and was minister of the East London Tabernacle, spoke on the Holy Spirit.[56] In 1949 the BRF published a call for the 'Opening of the Door to Mid-Century Revival'. Of the thirty people who had responsibility within the BRF, fifteen had been trained at Spurgeon's.[57] Later Philip Greenslade, who trained at Spurgeon's in the 1960s, became involved with Selwyn Hughes in leading Crusade for World Revival (CWR). Prayer for the spiritual revival of the church was part of the College tradition.

The call at the Keswick Convention and other places to a deeper spirituality also had an influence on the College constituency. Spurgeon was not a supporter of the Convention, but W.Y. Fullerton was one of those trained at the College in Spurgeon's time who was deeply affected by the Keswick message of full consecration and the filling of the Spirit. Keswick was central to British evangelicalism in the first half of the twentieth century. By the 1920s Fullerton, then Home Secretary of the BMS, was a leading Keswick speaker. In this period Graham Scroggie was remoulding Keswick thinking through his Convention Bible Readings.[58] The theme emphasised by Scroggie was making Christ Lord of one's life. Writing in 1925 in *The Christian*, Scroggie argued that Keswick teaching on the 'Spirit-filled' life was grounded in obedience to Christ's Lordship, which in his view was Keswick's distinctive message.[59] The emphasis on active obedience could become legalistic. Fullerton reflected a more activist outlook when he referred to the popular Keswick hymn 'Channels Only' and told his listeners that rather than simply being channels they should be God's living agents.[60] In 1938 Percy Evans spoke of the marked spiritual effect on the College through students who attended Keswick. Financial help was given from Keswick funds to one student to enable him to attend the Convention. Others attending received help from friends.[61] Geoffrey King, who gave public testimony at Keswick just before the war, and who indicated his indebtedness to Scroggie, was an important carrier of the message of consecration into the post-war years.[62] Raymond Brown, who wrote his PhD on holiness spirituality, was a regular speaker at Keswick and other conventions across the world.[63] From the 1960s Stanley Voke, who came from South Africa to study at the College in 1938, was known as a strong advocate of deeper spiritual experience.

In the 1960s Spurgeon's felt the impact of other movements of renewal – liturgical and charismatic. Stephen Winward, at Higham's Park, Walthamstow, gave lectures in the College on the minister's devotional life. He was deeply interested in renewal of worship and in particular the use of liturgy. In 1968 the College Council noted: 'A number of students (fourteen in all) have been influenced by the new Pentecostal teaching on the Holy Spirit.' The faculty members had spoken to the students and there had been discussion in College. The students involved were described as 'earnest, sincere and restrained'.[64] During the 1970s and 1980s charismatic spirituality had increasing influence in College. When Nigel Wright was appointed tutor in Christian Doctrine in 1987, he was known for having led Ansdell Baptist Church in significant growth and renewal. Paul Beasley-Murray considered that Wright's commitment to charismatic renewal would bring a healthy balance to Spurgeon's. The College, he emphasised, had connections with all areas of Baptist life and work – Baptist Union and non-Union, including charismatic groups.[65] Some former students, notably Henry Tyler and John Hosier, became involved in a new group led by Terry Virgo. A notable feature of this group, later known as New Frontiers, came to be its opposition to women in eldership.[66] Most of those trained at the College, however, were concerned to see renewal in broader terms. A survey of the student body conducted in 1989 showed, on the question of charismatic renewal, that 80% saw themselves as

College Group 1962
(George Beasley-Murray as Principal)

charismatic, 64% of the total claiming to have exercised the gift of tongues, 38% the gift of prophecy, and 13% the gift of healing.[67] The appointment of Nigel Wright as Principal in 2000 was an indictor of the way in which charismatic spirituality had found acceptance within the life of the College.

Interest in other streams of Christian spirituality also grew within the College. Students had always been encouraged to read the 'spiritual classics'. Spurgeon urged: 'Read Bunyan much; his *Holy War* for religious experience. Have *The Pilgrim's Progress* at your finger-ends.'[68] In the 1920s Quiet Days were led by F.B. Meyer, but the perception of students about their training in the first half of the century was that there was little knowledge of the Church's devotional literature or its mystical theology.[69] In 1988, through the leadership of Margaret Jarman, a former student at Spurgeon's, a Baptist Union Retreat Group was formed, and annual/termly retreat days were a feature of College life in this period. Peter Manson encouraged engagement with aspects of spirituality and students were increasingly introduced to the broad streams of Christian spiritual tradition. In 1990 Colin Brown, an Anglican who had taught at Avery Hill College and who had a particular interest in contemplative spirituality, was appointed to the full-time staff at Spurgeon's. Colin Brown, who became Academic Dean, introduced a module on Christian Spirituality within the College courses validated by the University of Wales. The teaching of spirituality was continued by Ian Randall, who joined the staff as Church History tutor in 1992. Topics with which students engage include evangelical spirituality, contemplative streams of spirituality, spiritual direction, charismatic traditions, black spirituality, women and spiritual experience, and spirituality and social action.[70]

Conclusion

Spirituality has always been seen as an important part of the training for ministry offered by the College. In 1889 Spurgeon said that students on leaving the College often observed: 'I feared that in coming to College I might lose my simplicity of faith and spirituality of mind; but there has been no danger in this place…I feel I have been greatly helped in the heavenly life.'[71] During Spurgeon's time the stress on spirituality was a notable feature of College life. For Spurgeon spirituality had to do with all aspects of life. A student or minister should not 'make his study a prison and his books the warders of a gaol, while nature lies outside his window calling him to health and beckoning him to joy.'[72] In the twentieth century a number of movements of revival and renewal which influenced the course of British evangelicalism affected the spiritual life of the College. Keswick spirituality had a huge impact on ministers such as Graham Scroggie. His inner conflict in ministry led to a fuller surrender and a more effective ministry.[73] This connection between spirituality and ministry came into focus in a more explicit way from the 1960s onwards. Over time the College came to the view that students should engage with a variety of streams of spirituality that would enable them to develop in their own spiritual journey and would undergird and enrich their ministries. In 1993 Michael Quicke, reiterating and affirming C.H. Spurgeon's strongly-held belief that the College should train effective preachers, also spoke of his own convictions about ministry – which included crucial elements such as preaching and vision, but which began with prayer.[74] Spiritual development was central to the College's vision.

1 *AP*, 1870, p. 4.

2 Ibid.

3 *S and T*, April 1870, p. 149.

4 Harte, *Historical Tablets*, pp. 21, 45.

5 *S and T*, March 1866, pp. 137-8.

6 *AP*, 1883-84, p. 6.

7 *S and T*, June 1880, pp. 254-6.

8 *S and T*, July 1880, p. 320.

9 *S and T*, June 1881, p. 303.

10 *S and T*, January 1866, pp. 41-3.

11 *AP*, 1870, p. 7; cf. D.W. Bebbington, 'Spurgeon and the common man', *Baptist Review of Theology*, Vol. 5, No. 1 (1995), pp. 63-75.

12 Spurgeon, *All-Round Ministry*, p. 47; *S and T*, May 1874, p. 223.

13 *AP*, 1870, p. 12.

14 Fullerton, *Spurgeon*, p. 233.

15 Spurgeon, *Lectures to my Students*, p. 172.

16 Fullerton, *Spurgeon*, p. 233.

17 *S and T*, June 1884, p. 295.

18 *AP*, 1901-02, pp. 5-7.

19 *S and T*, June 1906, p. 278.

20 *S and T*, January 1914, n.p., 'Concerning the College'.

21 *British Weekly*, 8 May 1924, p. 121; K.W. Clements, *Lovers of Discord: Twentieth-Century Theological Controversies in England* (London: SPCK, 1988), pp. 107-42.

22 See I.M. Randall, *English Baptists in the Twentieth Century* (Didcot: Baptist Historical Society, 2005), chapter 5.

23 Minutes of the Baptist Union Council, 24 and 25 November 1931.

24 Spurgeon, *Lectures to my Students*, p. 171.

25 *S and T*, June 1892, p. 279.

26 *S and T*, April 1901, pp. 160-1. C.F. Allison was a Deacon at the Tabernacle and Trustee of the College.

27 Nicholls, *Lights to the World*, pp. 140-2, for more details.

28 *College Record*, June 1965, pp. 31-2.

29 G. Holden Pike, *The Life and Work of Charles Haddon Spurgeon* (London: Cassell, n.d.), Vol. 2, pp. 287-8.

30 *The Keswick Week*, 1942, pp. 70-1; 1950, p. 192; 1954, pp. 5-6.

31 Fullerton, *Spurgeon*, p. 234.

32 *S and T*, April 1901, pp. 162-4.

33 *AP*, 1902-3, p. 6.

34 *College Annual Report*, 1935-36, p. 4.

35 *College Record*, April 1953, p. 16.

36 *S and T*, May 1874, p. 228; cf. *All-Round Ministry*, pp. 58-61.

37 *S and T*, May 1874, p. 229.

38 Spurgeon, *All-Round Ministry*, p. 49.

39 *College Record*, April 1949, pp. 3-4.

40 *S and T*, May 1882, pp. 261-2.

41 T.L. Johnson, *Twenty-Eight Years a Slave, or The Story of My Life in Three Continents* (Bournemouth: W. Mate & Sons, 1909), pp. 92-4.

42 *Spurgeon's College Magazine*, Midsummer 1941, p. 23.

43 Minutes of a Meeting of the Trustees of the College, 18 June 1896. (Box 6)

44 Minutes of a Meeting of the Trustees, 20 July 1896. Report of a meeting between F. Marchant and the President and Vice-President of the College: report held with Minutes of 20 July.

45 Minutes of a Special Meeting of Trustees, 30 July 1896; F. Marchant to Trustees, 16 February 1898.

46 Nicholls, *Lights to the World*, p. 152.

47 *S and T*, June 1881, p. 304.

48 *S and T*, May 1887, p. 210.

49 *College Record*, May 1955, p. 11.

50 Minutes of the Executive Committee, 10 December 1958; Minutes of College Council, 12 December 1958.

51 I am indebted to Debra Reid for her reflections on College chapel.

52 *AP*, 1904-5, pp. 3-4.

53 *AP*, 1904-5, pp. 7-8.

54 *Keswick Week*, 1921, pp. 242, 246; *S and T*, May 1922, pp. 361-2.

55 *The Baptist Revival Fellowship: Constitution and Rules* (London: BRF, n.d.): Spurgeon's College, London, BRF Archive, file TMB; cf. D.W. Bebbington, *Evangelicalism in Modern Britain: A History from the 1730s to the 1980s* (London: Routledge, 1995), pp. 230, 251.

56 *The Christian*, 30 April 1942, p. 3.

57 *Opening of the Door to Mid-Century Revival* (London: BRF, n.d.): BRF Archive, file TMB.

58 *S and T*, May 1939, p. 164.

59 *The Christian*, 23 July 1925, p. 6.

60 *Keswick Week*, 1924, pp. 165-6.

61 Minutes of College Council, 20 June 1938, p. 202. (Minute Book 1930-46, Box 6).

62 C. Price and I. Randall, *Transforming Keswick*, (Carlisle: Paternoster/OM, 2000), p. 77.

63 R. Brown, 'Evangelical Ideas of Perfection: A comparative study of the spirituality of men and movements in nineteenth century England', University of Cambridge PhD thesis, 1965.

64 Minutes of College Council, 9 April 1968.

65 Minutes of a College Council Conference, 9-10 January 1987

66 T. Virgo, *No Well-Worn Paths* (Eastbourne: Kingsway, 2001), pp. 301-3.

67 *BT*, 21 December 1989, p. 10.

68 Fullerton, *Spurgeon*, p. 235.

69 *College Record*, May 1955, pp. 7-12.

70 I.M. Randall, 'A deeper spirituality', *Talk*, Spring 2004, pp. 18-19.

71 *S and T*, June 1889, p. 311.

72 Spurgeon, *Lectures to my Students*, p. 172.

73 *Keswick Week*, 1921, p. 168; 1927, pp. 144-5; *The Keswick Convention*, 1930, pp. 128-9.

74 *College Record*, Autumn/Winter 1993, pp. 1-2.

Chapter 5: Connecting with the churches

In his book on the life of C.H. Spurgeon, W.Y. Fullerton described the increasing impact of the College on the churches. In 1861 there were twenty students, two years later there were sixty-six, and in some subsequent years there were more than a hundred. In 1866 the College had a third of the students in the nine Baptist colleges in the United Kingdom. In 1892, the year of Spurgeon's death, the College had trained nearly nine hundred students for the ministry. They had come from all parts of Britain - one was reputed to have walked all the way from the Highlands of Scotland - and increasingly from across the world.[1] The growth of the College had a profound impact on the churches, especially Baptist churches. Reports were received each year of numbers of those serving as Baptist pastors who had studied at the College, of the numbers in membership in their churches, of the number of baptisms that had been conducted by those pastors, and of the net contribution they had made to numerical Baptist growth. The College never saw itself as existing to do anything other than serve the churches and the wider work of mission. As it did so, it looked in turn to the churches for financial support. The College also began to influence the life of the Baptist Union and the larger Christian world. The first product of the College to become President of the Baptist Union was E.G. Gange, in 1897, and by the end of the Second World War eleven former students of the College had held this office. The College was an integral part of the wider life of the churches.

Serving the churches

George Rogers wrote in 1866 that many of the students who had trained at the College had succeeded in ministry in difficult situations where others had failed. Churches were certainly eager to have students from the College, seeing them as carrying the personal recommendation of Spurgeon. Because many of them came from the Metropolitan Tabernacle or associated churches, and because of the time he spent at the College, Spurgeon was able to take a personal interest in each student. Often he had a hand in their settlement process. Beyond that, the College fostered a continuing link with former students, offering, as Rogers put it, 'sympathy, counsel, and hope, in seasons of great difficulty and trial'.[2] In this early period there was great emphasis on planting churches in London. But students were called to serve churches in Essex, Hertfordshire, Buckinghamshire, Kent, Middlesex, Bedfordshire, Oxfordshire, Norfolk, Suffolk, Cambridgeshire, Northampton, Staffordshire, Warwickshire, Lincolnshire, Leicestershire, Derbyshire, Yorkshire, Durham, Lancashire, Gloucester, Huntingdon, Hampshire, Wiltshire, Somerset, Devon and Cornwall, as well as Wales, Scotland, Ireland and other countries. As one example, G.S. Neale went to Enon, Monkwearmouth, near Sunderland, in 1870, beginning his ministry with eleven people worshipping in a chapel seating 300. Within a year the chapel was filled. By 1873 the membership was seventy and there were plans to extend the chapel, which was apparently the only Baptist cause in an area with a population of 30,000 people.[3]

In June 1881 *The Sword and the Trowel* could speak of 355 former students in ministry, and it noted that some were 'in the more prominent pulpits of the denomination'. But the main concern of the College was to serve the churches

Shoreditch Tabernacle Interior

as a whole. The report spoke of pastors that had been trained at the College who were 'in positions where their patience and self-denial are severely tested by the present depression in trade, and the consequent inability of rural congregations to furnish them with adequate support.' The College was delighted by 'the success of her most honoured sons', but was equally determined to affirm 'the faithfulness and perseverance of the rank and file'.[4] A year later, however, attention was again drawn to some of the 'leading pastors' who had been students in the College. Clearly there was a good deal of pride in their achievements. In London several were building up flourishing congregations, and significant work was also being done elsewhere. Among those mentioned were: A.G. Brown at the East London Tabernacle, which had a congregation of over 3,000; William Cuff, with his pioneering work at the Shoreditch Tabernacle; C.B. Sawday at King's Cross; Frank White at Lower Sloane Street, Chelsea (later at the Talbot Tabernacle, Bayswater); George Hill, at South Parade Baptist Church, Leeds; E.G. Gange, minister at Broadmead, Bristol (later at Regent's Park Chapel, London); and T.G. Tarn, who was called to St Andrew's Street, Cambridge, when in his twenties.[5] Broadmead and St Andrew's Street were among the most prestigious churches in the Baptist Union.

By this time, however, there were also former students who had lost connection with Christian ministry. 'We have', said Spurgeon in 1885, 'our failures to deplore'.[6] One example was Francis Ward Monck, the eighth student accepted by Spurgeon into the College, in 1859. He had short ministries in Northamptonshire, Yorkshire, Staffordshire and Hampshire, and in 1873 he settled at Totterdown, Bristol, where he became friendly with F.R. Young, a Baptist minister in Swindon who had embraced spiritualism and the role of mediums. Monck described in 1876 how 'spirits' began to give him his text when he preached, and 'controlling his vocal organ caused him to discourse logically and eloquently upon it'. Loud raps were heard on the floor of his church. Not surprisingly, Monck's congregation and fellow ministers turned against him. Monck decided that his Baptist ministry had ended when his chapel was burned down. From then on he became a travelling medium, and claimed that another former student at the College, Samuel Wheeler, who had died in 1869 when in his late twenties, was his spirit guide.[7] Another

Woolwich Tabernacle

student who left evangelical ministry was C. Spurgeon Medhurst, the son of Thomas Medhurst. In 1882 C.S. Medhurst was preaching 'with much acceptance' in Woolwich, where there was a strong Baptist witness.[8] He became a missionary in China, but left this ministry and became involved in Theosophy, writing for Annie Besant's *Adyar Bulletin* and working with another leading theosophist, Charles Leadbeater.[9]

Despite some disappointments, the picture up to the early twentieth century was of progress in many churches with College-trained ministers - Frank Smith at Ilford, J.E. Martin at Erith, F.W. Porter at Bexleyheath, J.R. Edwards at Kenyon, and John Wilson at the Woolwich Tabernacle. In 1915, when the first Area Superintendents were appointed to serve the churches of the Baptist Union, five of them had trained at the College. One, J.W. Ewing, was referred to by a colleague in the LBA as 'the greatly loved Baptist Bishop of London'.[10] In 1932 M.E. Aubrey, the Baptist Union General Secretary, applauded the passion exhibited by John Wilson, William Cuff and J.C. Carlile in their long and fruitful ministries.[11] Spurgeon's also continued in

Student group 1907-1911

the inter-war years to produce those who would have particularly significant pastoral ministries: Ernest Peskett at Denmark Place, Camberwell; Sidlow Baxter at Charlotte Chapel, Edinburgh; Geoffrey King at the East London Tabernacle; Leslie Larwood at the Tabernacle, Stockton-on-Tees, and the West Croydon Tabernacle; J.J. Brown in Erith and Dagenham; George Cumming at Victoria, Eastbourne; J.T. Hamilton at Richmond,

Student group 1930-1934

Liverpool; Godfrey Robinson at Main Road, Romford, and Park Road, Bromley; and Stanley Voke at Bethesda in Sunderland, Upton Vale in Torquay, and Walton-on-Thames. J.J. Brown and George Cumming were both chairmen of the College Council. Although student numbers in College in this period were rarely more than forty, much less than in Spurgeon's time, the impact of the students was considerable.

The years after the Second World War saw an upsurge in those offering for ministry and also a strong commitment to evangelism. A mission in Blackheath in 1947, led by J.J. Brown, who served in Erith, in Dagenham (leading the group of Baptist churches), and as College Secretary, involved typical activities: house-to-house visiting, factory work, speaking to people in pubs, and children's services. Brown was assisted by two students, Ron Luland, later a leader in the BRF, and Donald Cranefield, who was to have significant ministries in Southall and Bromley.[12] Many such College missions were held. In April 1954, one student, Douglas Sparkes, who

Student group 1948-1952

would exercise wider ministry in the Baptist denomination, wrote an 'open letter' to ministers outlining how College students were serving the churches. Over one year students had held missions, fulfilled nearly 1,300 Sunday preaching engagements, served as camp chaplains, and spoken at conferences. Sparkes said it had been 'a real thrill to see decisions made for Christ and to know the up-building of His Church'.[13] Students trained in the 1940s and 1950s again included a number whose pastoral work would become well known: Eric Hayden at the Metropolitan Tabernacle; Arthur Thompson at Ruislip; Reg Dalton at West Wickham and Shirley; C.J.W. Doble at Holland Road, Hove; Chris Norrish in Chelmsford; Raymond Brown at Zion, Cambridge, and Upton Vale, Torquay; Colin Marchant in West Ham; Robert Archer in Canterbury; Norman Moss at Queen's Road, Wimbledon; and Tom Rogers in Gillingham. A number developed wider ministries. The emphasis remained, however, on Spurgeon's as a College training pastors.

College Conference

In a report in 1867, George Rogers stated that the connection of students with the College was fostered through a 'bond of union'.[14] This union was officially entitled the Pastors' College Association, often shortened to College Conference since its best-known expression was an annual conference held, usually for a week in March, at the College and the Metropolitan Tabernacle. The College conference hall was used for the ministers' sessions of the Conference and traditionally the wives of ministers sat in the gallery. Larger open meetings were held in the Tabernacle. At the first Conference about 140 ministers were present, and about 40 students were welcomed into the Association.[15] The basis of agreement of the Association was 'first – upon the doctrines of grace; secondly, upon believer's baptism; and thirdly, upon earnest endeavours to win souls to Christ'.[16] Conference numbers later exceeded 400. For some pastors this week was their only break from ministry. The Conference always began with an hour of open prayer and a full programme of addresses followed - at one early conference twenty-eight addresses were delivered. Hymns were sung, led by a precentor, since Spurgeon was not in favour of musical instruments. The College Anthem was 'Hallelujah for the Cross'. The high point of

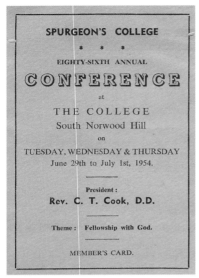

Spurgeon's College Conference Programme 1954

Spurgeon's College Speech Day 1961

the Conference was always the address by Spurgeon, when Conference rose and cheered 'the governor'. At the end of the week the Lord's Supper was celebrated.[17] Conference finished with the singing of Psalm 122 - 'Pray that Jerusalem may have peace and felicity'. 'At the last verse', one minister remarked, 'the grip of the hand is tightened, and the electric current of sympathy passes all along the ranks.'[18] Conference members went home with a strong sense of being bound together in fellowship.

A number of special events were associated with the Conference. One was the public meeting at which well-known visitors were usually invited as speakers so that ministers, students and others could hear them. In 1874, for example, Thomas Barnardo, famed for his welfare work with children, was a speaker, as was Danzy Sheen, a Primitive Methodist minister who had trained at the College.[19] Walter Mayers, a College student and then a pastor, later joined Barnardo's work. In 1875 Spurgeon invited D.L. Moody and Ira Sankey, who were reaching the end of their two-year campaign in Britain, to take part in the public meeting. They were enabled, said the report of the Conference, to 'stimulate every one to holy zeal'.[20] Before the public meeting a tea was provided at the Tabernacle. Often 4,000 people came to the public meeting and half of this number came to the tea beforehand. Visits might also be made to other 'Spurgeonic' churches in London. Special arrangements were made for meals for Conference members during the week. Spurgeon's wife, Susannah (usually known as Susie), established a tradition by which she presented each of the ministers at the Conference with a book which she chose and which she paid for out of the Book Fund which she administered. In 1883, referring to a copy of a new book by her husband which she had presented to Conference members, she said she hoped that the book would be a 'true helpmeet' to them.[21] The Spurgeons also had groups of ministers to their home, 'Westwood', in South Norwood. At the 1894 Conference, two years after Spurgeon's death, Susannah was compared with Catherine Booth, the 'mother of the [Salvation] Army'. Mrs Spurgeon was described as 'the mother of the College and the mother of the Conference'.[22]

After Spurgeon's death the atmosphere at the Conference was not as electric as it had been under Spurgeon's leadership, and numbers attending were much lower. The numbers of those trained at the College and actively engaged in ministry as pastors, missionaries and evangelists was almost 700 by the 1890s. Not all of these were Conference members, but at that stage the Conference was also open to associates. Despite this, the numbers attending on some occasions in the 1890s could be as low as 120. There was hope for fresh impetus when Thomas Spurgeon became President of College Conference in 1895. The conference hall was full for his inaugural address. Three years later he received the bad news, while the 1898 College Conference was in session, that the Metropolitan Tabernacle was on fire. It had to be rebuilt, which took two years. Susannah Spurgeon, the 'Mother of the College', remained active during this period. When she died in 1903 A.G. Brown described her as a 'minister to the ministry'.[23] The 1905 Conference, following the Welsh Revival, was described as a Revival Conference,[24] but generally there was little alteration in routine. In the early decades of the twentieth century the format of Conference, and even the hymns sung, remained substantially as they had been under Spurgeon. As an example of the reluctance to introduce change, one Conference member, Fred King, was song precentor for half a century, from 1902. The main changes were in Conference speakers. Percy Evans had many contacts and invited speakers from different denominations to Conference.[25]

Cartoon showing Spurgeon linked with Moody and Sankey

Mrs Susannah Spurgeon

Change gradually came. The Conference was reduced to two days and it came to be associated with the end of year event at which students were commissioned - what was called Speech Day and then later Open Day. Each year a new President of Conference was elected and some introduced new ideas. In

Spurgeon and deacons of the Metropoltan Tabernacle 1878

the 1950s speech day attracted 800 people, who were housed in a marquee on the lawn, and when the day was moved from Thursday to Saturday numbers rose to 1,000. Students were encouraged by the support forthcoming from their home churches. However, just as the numbers at Conference had declined, so gradually reducing numbers at the Open Day meant that it no longer made economic sense to hire a marquee. From 2002 a new pattern was adopted: a combined event, bringing together graduation and commissioning of students, was held in the Ashcroft Theatre, central Croydon. In addition to the annual Conference, now held on only one day, connection between the College and those in ministry has been fostered by weekly prayer in the Chapel for former students – Conference prayers.

Over the course of a cycle of six or seven years all students are written to (six each week) and asked for news which can be the focus of prayer. Former students also meet in large numbers for a College Reunion each year during the Baptist Assembly and some student batches keep in close touch. The College still adheres to the vision set out by George Rogers in 1867 – a 'Union' that fosters communication after students have left the College and helps ministers, as Rogers put it, 'to perform the full duties of the pastorate'.[26]

Finance and administration

College Conference, as it operated in the nineteenth century, also served as an important means of raising funds for the College. From the beginning a variety of means were used to generate money to support the work. In the early period, when the number of students was small and there was no separate College building, Spurgeon financed the project from, as he put it, 'the large sale of my sermons in America, together with my dear wife's economy'. At that time the outlay on the College was £600 to £800 in a year. However, Spurgeon denounced the continuance of slavery in the United States, publicly calling it 'a crime of crimes', and as a result his sermons were boycotted in the Southern states.[27] Other sources of finance had to be found. One of the Deacons at the Tabernacle, W.C. Murrell, of 'The Lawn', South Lambeth, took responsibility for a weekly offering at the Tabernacle on behalf of the College. Offerings had been taken previously but they were, according to Spurgeon, 'meagre'. Under Murrell a new approach was evident. By dint of some manipulation, in 1869 the amount given reached exactly £1869.[28] Another deacon,

T.R. Phillips, undertook to provide a supper, during Conference week, for donors, and this became the single largest source of income for the College. There was reference to 400 people enjoying a 'sumptuous supper' and to the 'exquisite taste and unrivalled hospitality' of Phillips. Guests then promised large donations.[29] Often over £2,000 was raised during Conference week.

The College and the Metropolitan Tabernacle had wealthy supporters, such as Joseph Passmore, of Spurgeon's publisher, Passmore and Alabaster, who was a deacon of the Tabernacle and a Trustee of the College. Another deacon and Trustee was William Higgs, a successful builder who was very generous to Spurgeonic causes. Very large amounts of money were given for chapel-building.[30] But other supporters were equally valued by the College. Mrs Lavinia Bartlett, who led a Bible Class for 700 young women at the Tabernacle, and who was regarded by Spurgeon as 'his right-hand supporter in Christian labour', made the College the main focus of money raised by the class.[31] The members of the class raised money in various ways and in addition held a half-yearly tea on behalf of the College. The College students attended and, 'with their usual cheerful zeal' (as one report put it), acted as waiters. A cheque was then presented to the College. Spurgeon would speak and the formidable Mrs Bartlett would give an address which was strongly evangelistic. In 1868, for example, after praying at the end of her address, she pronounced: 'Lord, thou hast heard

C.H.Spurgeon and Joseph Passmore

Mrs Lavinia Bartlett

us: souls are saved this night!'[32] Spurgeon also encouraged churches to support students, especially students who served churches as preachers. An article in 1866, by 'A Friend to Students', probably written by Spurgeon, urged the churches to think about their financial responsibilities to students. The article condemned deacons who 'proffered' a 'pittance', and it urged a more generous attitude.[33]

Even in Spurgeon's time the income generated for the College was insufficient and legacies made up the shortfall. This problem became more acute later. The amount collected at the 1893 Conference was £1,500, the smallest figure since 1871, and further decline followed. Matters such as investments continued to be handled by James Spurgeon, who had great financial acumen, and a College financial committee operated, made up of businessmen who were deacons at the Tabernacle. A Life Assurance scheme was launched, making provision for the families of deceased ministers. Gradually, however, arrangements changed, particularly after James Spurgeon's death in 1900.[34] The College was losing momentum. As an example, Thomas Spurgeon reported that 1903-4 had been 'comparatively uneventful'.[35] From 1917 a new framework for the College was put in place, with Trustees being elected by College Conference, and this gave way to an elected College Council, with John Bradford as chairman. Bradford had trained at the College in the 1870s, was minister of Fairlop Road, Leytonstone, and Secretary of the London Baptist Association in the early twentieth century, and then became a successful businessman.[36] The hope was to find better ways to connect with the wider College constituency and to find a more secure financial footing. Percy Evans, as Principal, worked closely with Thomas Greenwood, who trained in the 1870s, had pastorates in London (at Catford Hill and Ramsden Road, Balham), and was Council chairman from 1926 to 1935, and also with F.J.H. Humphrey, chairman from 1935 to 1947.[37] A.H. Philpot, OBE, who was on the College Council in the 1950s and 1960s, was a generous benefactor. Concern to find ways to support the College financially through connections with churches and individuals has continued.

The College Secretary has traditionally had the main administrative responsibility for College affairs, including finance. During C.H. Spurgeon's time and up to the First World War the secretaryship was filled by someone associated with the Tabernacle, and the College office remained at the Tabernacle until 1938. From 1916 until 1924, John Weeks, who had served with the BMS in Congo after training at the College, was College Secretary, and he was followed by Ernest Welton, who also served as pastor at Honor Oak. G.W. Harte, minister at Elm Road, Beckenham, became Secretary in 1937 and brought about considerable improvement in the management of the College.[38] Changes continued under successive secretaries – Geoffrey Rusling (the church history tutor), A.E. Wilmott (minister at West Ealing), Wilfrid Roper, J.J. Brown and David Harrison. Considerable help was given by honorary treasurers. Financial help for the work of the College has been and is received from many churches, individuals and funds, notably the Particular Baptist Fund.[39] With the appointment of Paul Scott-Evans - a banker and then the Executive Director of Youth for Christ - as College business manager, the management of College life, which includes public relations and a significant responsibility for fund-raising as well as internal administration, was considerably strengthened. The current arrangement has echoes of how the College operated under James Spurgeon, who, as J.C. Carlile put it, 'had charge of all the business arrangements of the College'.[40]

The College and the Baptist Union

C.H. Spurgeon was a convinced Baptist, and the College's denominational links were almost entirely with Baptist churches and associations. Certainly Spurgeon had a wider vision of the Christian Church, and preached in churches of several denominations, but he never saw the College as inter-denominational. In 1882, when he looked back at a quarter of a century of training, he identified 464 former students serving as pastors, missionaries and evangelists, twenty-eight in other Christian service, thirteen in secular work, seven in medical mission, and only two specifically educated for other denominations. Some former students were, however, now in other denominations, and some had changed their views about baptism - which astounded Spurgeon.[41] Often Spurgeon was involved, with his brother James, in seeking to place students in churches after their training, functioning rather as Area Superintendents would in the twentieth century.[42] Although, as we will see in chapter 8, Spurgeon withdrew from the Baptist Union during the 'Down Grade controversy' (1887-88), the vast bulk of his ministry was within the orbit of the Union. Even after Spurgeon withdrew from the Union, the tradition continued that students who were leaving the College went into Union churches as pastors - or went overseas. The College-trained ministers who became Baptist Union Presidents up to the Second World War were: E.G. Gange, William Cuff, John Wilson, J.W. Ewing, Charles Joseph, W.Y. Fullerton, D.J. Hiley, J.C. Carlile, Gilbert Laws, F.J.H. Humphrey, and Percy Evans.[43] James Spurgeon was elected President but died before taking office. All of these ministers were known as effective preachers and pastors.

Because of the College's strong links with Baptist life, it was to other Baptists that Spurgeon and the College leadership primarily looked for support, including financial support. At the 1866 fund-raising dinner for the College the chairman was William Brock, minister of Bloomsbury Chapel, with whom Spurgeon had co-operated closely in founding the London Baptist Association. Also present was Sir Morton Peto, MP, a well-known Baptist and a Victorian entrepreneur who was involved in many construction projects – for example, Nelson's column. After Spurgeon gave a speech in which he described the work that had been done through the College as 'second to none in the kingdom', William Brock referred to this 'marvellous account' by Spurgeon and made the quite remarkable suggestion that it was doubtful whether such an account had been heard in any part of the earth since the days of the apostles. The stress during the evening was on the supply of ministers for new and existing Baptist churches. James Spurgeon stated that of fifty-nine newly trained pastors taking Baptist churches twenty-four were from the Pastors' College.[44] This could have been taken as an exercise in self-congratulation, and to some extent that was the case. However, Spurgeon did establish relationships with other Colleges. In 1882, for example, Spurgeon presided at the communion service at Regent's Park College and it was reported that he had enjoyed 'a happy time' with the Principal, Joseph Angus.[45]

Concerns were raised from time to time about over-supply of ministers within the Baptist Union. Was the Pastors' College, by producing so many ministers, contributing to this problem? In 1883 Spurgeon responded by suggesting that there were people already in the ministry who should not be there. 'We are overdone with mediocrity,' he stated, 'and the grades below that poor level. We feel sure that many have mistaken their calling: we should not have so many preachers and so little good preaching if the divine call had been waited for.' For his part, Spurgeon made clear, he discouraged unsuitable people from ministry. He also commended bi-vocational ministry. 'We know', he said, 'a very useful minister who at a pinch peddled maps, another to this day serves as a clerk, a third helps in the harvest-field, and a fourth sells books and does colporteur's work. Why not?'[46] Spurgeon insisted that those trained at the College readily settled in churches.[47] The course at the College was lengthened to address worries about over-supply of ministers, but Spurgeon continued to seek to refute charges that the number of unemployed ministers had increased because of the numbers trained at the College.[48] McCaig continued the defence of the College. In 1906 he said: 'The College has sent out many men who have filled high places in the denomination, while not less faithful men have successfully occupied the difficult and lonely rural posts.' Ministers with ability were needed in the 'rising watering places', such as coastal towns, he argued, and in such places the majority of the Baptist churches were led by ministers from the College.[49]

Denominational issues recurred. Before the First World War, J.H. Shakespeare, Union General Secretary, hoped to draw the Baptist colleges closer together, but the Pastors' College stated flatly that it opposed interference with its 'absolute and sole authority in the matter of the choice and training of the students of the Pastors' College'.[50] In 1928 the College Council complained to M.E. Aubrey, Shakespeare's successor, about a Union proposal to make passing a medical examination a condition for being an accredited minister and spoke (with Spurgeon in mind?) of the contribution of 'men of frail physique'.[51] The real objection was to centralisation. Despite these tensions, in 1938 it was agreed that the College should affiliate to the Union. Evans pointed out that most former students served in the Union or the BMS. Eleven members of College Council were on the Baptist Union Council. F.J. Walkey, who trained at the College in the 1890s and who received the Military Cross and the OBE for his First World War chaplaincy work, was Central Area Superintendent for twenty-two years and chaired College Council.[53] When Percy Evans was elected Union President for 1940/41 *The Sword and the Trowel* praised the denomination for entrusting leadership to someone combining 'scholarship with Evangelical fervour'.[54] In 1946 Ernest Payne, later Union General Secretary, welcomed the first conference for Baptist colleges' staff.[55] Wider Spurgeon's involvement in the Union continued. George Beasley-Murray was Union President in 1968, J.J. Brown in 1972 (following the death of Godfrey Robinson, also Spurgeon's-trained), and George Cumming in 1974. In the 1980s David Coffey (1986), Margaret Jarman (1987) and Colin Marchant (1988) were Presidents, followed later by Steve Gaukroger (1994), Fred George (1997), Nigel Wright (2002) and Peter Manson (2004).[56] David Coffey, after ministry at Upton Vale, Torquay, became Union Secretary for Evangelism, and, in 1991, General Secretary.

Wider connections

Although Spurgeon wished to see the Baptist denomination flourish, he also nurtured other connections as a way of helping the College. The breadth of Spurgeon's ecclesiastical sympathies is illustrated by the fact that he appointed George Rogers, an Independent minister – and so someone holding paedobaptist views - as the first College Principal. They had many good-natured disagreements.[57] At the annual College Conference supporters' evening dinner, non-Baptists often took a prominent part. The 1869 evening, for example, was presided over by the MP for Cambridge, who also spoke, and the MP for Marylebone was another speaker.[58] This kind of pattern continued. At the 1886 Conference there were prominent Baptist ministers among the speakers - Charles Williams, the President-elect of the Baptist Union 'spoke with much power upon the resemblance which should exist between our ministry, and that of the Lord Jesus Christ' – but at the meeting at which money was raised addresses were given by an Anglican, Canon Fleming, and an MP, Thomas Blake.[59] Often these events also featured well-known singers, such as Annie Ryall. In 1890 George Williams of the YMCA presided at the fund-raising evening, with Sir John Kennaway, the President of (the Anglican) Church Missionary Society being one of the speakers. There was reference to the connection between the College and the YMCA.[60] Throughout its history College Conference has drawn speakers from a wide variety of backgrounds.

Wider connections were also formed through ministries beyond the churches, some socially orientated. A notable example was the Orphanage (later Spurgeon's Child Care). In 1914, with the outbreak of war, three College students enlisted in the Royal Army Medical Corps. The YMCA link was again important. Five students began to conduct meetings in army camps under the auspices of YMCA.[61] Determined representations by J.H. Shakespeare and R.J. Wells, Secretary of the Congregational Union, led to Baptist and Congregational pastors being accepted as chaplains, under a United Navy and Army Board.[62] F.J.H. Humphrey, an early Baptist chaplain to the troops, served in Baghdad. He became Assistant Principal Chaplain and received the DSO. After the war Humphrey was minister at the well-known Baptist church, St Mary's, Norwich. Another former College student, Arthur John Potts, who came to College in 1927, became a Principal Chaplain in the RAF.[63] The trend for ministers trained at the College to take on chaplaincies was a significant feature from the 1960s. As examples, G.V. Whitefield, who was at College in the

1950s, became a University chaplain in the 1970s, and Ian McFarlane was a chaplain to HM Forces in the 1980s, and later (when senior minister at Bookham) Secretary to the United Board. In the 1990s others became known for their hospital and military chaplaincy: Peter Clarke, for instance, as chaplain to Mildmay Mission Hospital, and Jonathan Woodhouse as chaplain to the Forces.

The world Baptist community itself offered the College opportunities for contacts. At the Baptist World Alliance (BWA) Congress in Stockholm in 1923, Gilbert Laws, who was the chairman of the British Baptist Continental Committee, called for Baptist denominational self-consciousness, emphasizing the importance of conversion, churches based on the New Testament, and believer's baptism.[64] After the Second World War College involvement in international Baptist affairs increased. George Beasley-Murray addressed BWA meetings, and from the 1980s there was considerable involvement by College principals in the BWA. Paul Beasley-Murray had a particular interest in Europe, as well as serving on BWA Commissions. Michael Quicke was heavily engaged with world Baptist affairs, and Nigel Wright became chairman of the BWA Study Commission on Christian Ethics. There were also many European contacts from the mid-twentieth century. Pat Rose was the first English student to spend a year at the recently-established Baptist Theological Seminary at Rüschlikon, Switzerland. He reported in 1954 that he had discovered the variety of Baptist life – Scandinavian Baptists who tended towards Pentecostal spirituality, Russians who were Pietist, German and Dutch who were 'born theologians', Americans who were Fundamentalist and 'the odd Englishman' trying to be 'all things to all men'.[65] In 1957 a Conference of European Baptist Tutors was held in Rüschlikon and this became a regular event through which tutors at Spurgeon's and the other British Colleges connected with their counterparts across Europe.

Finally, representatives of the College were involved in ecumenical affairs. In 1945 the Archbishop of Canterbury, Geoffrey Fisher, drew together Anglican and Free Church leaders for ecumenical theological discussions. Percy Evans was one of four Baptist representatives in these talks, helping to produce a book, *The Catholicity of Protestantism*. Three years later Evans was one of a small group from the Baptist Union appointed to represent the Union at the formation of the World Council of Churches (WCC) in Amsterdam. Indeed in 1948 Evans attended the Lambeth Conference, the Methodist Conference and the WCC Assembly.[66] Many evangelicals opposed involvement in the WCC, and against this background George Beasley-Murray, a participant in WCC study groups, wrote in 1955 about the WCC from an evangelical perspective. He strongly commended one WCC paper - Christ the Hope of the World – as one of the finest declarations on eschatology he had read, stating: 'I should be grateful to God if the general theology of the World Council of Churches, and the deep spirituality manifested therein, characterised our own Denomination. In fact, we fall far short of it.'[67] Under Beasley-Murray a tradition was established of exchanging six College students for a week with the Anglican

Lincoln Theological College. Writing in 1963, C.T. Cook said that compared with 1913, when he started as a minister, it was good to see the breaking down of barriers between Anglican and Free Church life.[68] Roger Nunn, who trained at the College in the 1960s, held posts with the British Council of Churches and Churches Together in England until his retirement in 2001. By then the College had become a place that attracted people of all denominations.

Conclusion

There has been something of a tension in the relationship of the College to the wider Baptist community. The 'school of the prophets' has sought to express a critical loyalty. In the early period Spurgeon was concerned to renew Baptist life. He was delighted in 1873 to be able to report that ministers educated at the College were 'now occupying leading positions in the denomination'.[69] It was primarily from Baptists that he looked for support. Yet it was reported in 1915 that money that might have been given to the College was being withheld because the College would not 'fall into line with the denominational institutions'. The background was J.H. Shakespeare's drive for denominational centralisation. The forthright view taken by McCaig in 1915 was that 'our plans are distinct, our operations are uncontrolled, and we are an entirely independent institution…and we do not intend to be trammelled by any coalition, amalgamation, committee or clique'.[70] Percy Evans was able to connect the College more strongly with the Union. Despite this, Spurgeon's could still be at odds with Union thinking. When there was discussion within the Union in 1966 about having a central selection conference for those applying for ministry, Spurgeon's objected, and the selection scheme was limited to non-collegiate students.[71] Independent thinking has continued, but as we will see in the next chapter the College has increasingly embraced opportunities for ministry in the wide constituency it serves. Increasingly connections with the churches have been transdenominational. Paddy Mallon, who trained in the 1980s, became one of the ministers at St Thomas, Sheffield, an Anglican-Baptist partnership, which was one of the largest churches in the country. In the year 2000 Nigel Wright spoke about coming to the College as Principal 'with a strong sense of what this institution can contribute to the Christian church, to the evangelical movement, to the Baptist tradition here and overseas and to the lifelong training of attractive and evangelical ministers of the Gospel'.[72]

1   Fullerton, *Spurgeon*, pp. 230-1.

2   *S and T*, January 1866, p. 43; March, 1866, p. 137.

3   *S and T*, February 1873, pp. 88-9.

4   *S and T*, June 1881, p. 304.

5   *S and T*, May 1882, p. 262.

6   *AP*, 1884-85, p. 5.

7   J.L. Randall, 'Francis Ward Monck and the Problems of Physical Mediumship', *Journal of the Society for Psychical Research*, Vol. 67, No. 4 (2003), pp. 243-59.

8   *S and T*, August 1882, pp. 598-9.

9   J.C. Carlile, *My Life's Little Day* (London: Blackie, 1935), pp. 60-1. Carlile states that C.S. Medhurst joined the Old Catholic Church, but this seems unlikely. Leadbeater and some other theosophists were priests in the Liberal Catholic Church, established in 1916, and it is probably this which Medhurst joined.

10 *AP*, 1921-22, p. 4.

11 M.E. Aubrey to T.R. Glover, 13 March 1932, cited by W.M.S. West, 'The Reverend Secretary Aubrey: Part 1', *Baptist Quarterly [BQ]*, Vol. 34, No 5 (1992), p. 203.

12 *Spurgeon's College Magazine*, Autumn 1947.

13 *Spurgeon's College Record*, April 1954, p. 29.

14 *Outline* (1867), p. 16.

15 *S and T*, May 1865, p. 229.

16 *Outline* (1867), p. 45.

17 See I.M. Randall and T. Grass, 'C.H. Spurgeon on the Sacraments', in A. Cross, ed., *Baptist Sacramentalism* (Carlisle: Paternoster Press, 2003), pp. 55-75.

18 *S and T*, June 1891, p. 337.

19 D. Sheen, *Pastor C.H. Spurgeon* (London: J.B. Knapp, 1892), pp. 85-6.

20 *S and T*, May 1875, p. 240.

21 *S and T*, May 1883, p. 251. For the Book Fund see S. Spurgeon, *Ten Years of my Life: In the service of the Book Fund* (London: Passmore and Alabaster, 1886), and *Ten Years After* (London: Passmore and Alabaster, 1895).

22 *S and T*, June 1894, p. 284.

23 *S and T*, December 1903, p. 602.

24 *S and T*, June 1905, p. 285.

25 *Spurgeon's College Report*, 1949, p. 11.

26 Rogers, 'Outline', in *Outline* (1867), pp. 16, 25.

27 Carlile, *Spurgeon*, pp. 159-61.

28 *S and T*, April 1870, pp. 146-7.

29 *S and T*, April 1866, pp. 189, 191.

30 *S and T*, April 1870, p. 148

31 *S and T*, October 1865, pp. 466-7; cf. Spurgeon, *Autobiography*, Vol. 3, p. 36. Mrs Bartlett is referred to as Mrs Bondit in Drummond, *Spurgeon: Prince of Preachers*, p. 476.

32 *S and T*, January 1868, p. 44.

33 *S and T*, October 1866, pp. 460-3.

34 See Appendix 2 by P. Scott-Evans for more on the finances.

35 *AP*, 1903-4, p. 5.

36 W.C. Johnson, *Encounter in London: The Story of the London Baptist Association, 1865-1965* (London: Carey Kingsgate Press, 1965), p. 58.

37 *Spurgeon's College Report*, 1949, p. 7.

38 Nicholls, *Lights to the World*, pp. 160-1.

39 See T. Valentine, *Concern for the Ministry* (Teddington: Particular Baptist Fund, 1967), pp. v, vi, 41.

40 Carlile, *Life's Little Day*, p. 61.

41 *S and T*, May 1882, p. 262.

42 Bebbington, 'Spurgeon and British Evangelical Theological Education', p. 227.

43 E.A. Payne, *The Baptist Union: A Short History* (London: Baptist Union, 1958), pp. 259-61.

44 *S and T*, April 1866, pp. 190-1.

45 *S and T*, July 1882, p. 379.

46 *S and T*, March 1883, pp. 109-10.

47 *AP*, 1885-86, p. 27.

48 *S and T*, June 1891, p. 334.

49 *S and T*, June 1906, p. 278.

50 Minutes of College Council, 4 March 1909; see Nicholls, *Lights to the World*, p. 124, and P. Shepherd, *The Making of a Modern Denomination: John Howard Shakespeare and the English Baptists, 1898-1924* (Carlisle: Paternoster Press, 2001), p. 66.

51 Minutes of College Council, 25 October 1928.

52 Minutes of College Council, 15 December 1938.

53 For further information on Superintendents, see chapter 6.

54 *S and T*, June 1939, p. 187.

55 *Spurgeon's College Magazine*, Spring 1946, p. 3.

56 Peter Manson was trained at the South Wales Baptist College.

57 Fullerton, *Spurgeon*, p. 230.

58 *S and T*, April 1869, p. 190.

59 *S and T*, June 1886, pp. 296-7.

60 *S and T*, June 1890, p. 288.

61 *S and T*, 1913-14, p. 58.

62 See Shepherd, *The Making of a Modern Denomination*, pp. 96-103.

63 *College Record*, December 1962, pp. 16-17.

64 *BT*, 20 July 1923, pp. 518-20; 27 July 1923, p. 542.

65 *College Record*, April 1954, pp. 7-8.

66 *Spurgeon's College Students' Magazine*, Christmas 1948, pp. 8-9.

67 *BT*, 29 December 1955, p. 6.

68 *College Record*, June 1963, p. 5.

69 *S and T*, March 1873, p. 141.

70 *AP*, 1915-16, p. 5.

71 Minutes of College Council, 22-23 March 1966.

72 *College Record*, November 2000, p. 2

Chapter 6: Opening up opportunities

Writing in 1891, near the end of his life, C.H. Spurgeon gave an account of how the College had trained 845 students for 'the sacred ministry'. Spurgeon emphasised that although some of the students had previously received 'a high-class secular education', most had come to College 'with very deficient learning, or none at all'. This was not accidental. Spurgeon's vision from the beginning had been to offer opportunities in his 'school of the prophets' to those 'who had not been able to secure a sufficient education in their earlier days.' Those who had early educational advantages were welcome, since they still needed 'Biblical instruction, and guidance as to the duties of the pulpit and the pastorate', but the College felt a special responsibility to the disadvantaged. 'We opened a door of hope', said Spurgeon, 'for those who could not pass an examination in the standards of scholarship, but yet had been used of the Lord in the winning of souls.' The College had now been operating for thirty-five years, and although there were changes in the average educational level of the students Spurgeon was as firmly committed as ever to the opening of opportunities to those 'for whom our classes were first formed'.[1] Spurgeon also referred frequently to the fact that a major objective had been to help those who could not afford an education.[2] By the twentieth century changes were evident. The educational background of students was higher and more students could contribute to the cost of their training. Later in the century the College began to offer a range of possibilities in areas such as part-time training and continuing development as a resource for ministers. The College became more diverse and new opportunities for study continued to emerge.

Access to education

Although Spurgeon spoke in terms of 'opening a door of hope', this did not mean that there was open access for all. Applicants were carefully vetted, usually by Spurgeon himself. In reply to one applicant in 1874, Spurgeon noted that the signatures of his referees seemed to be written in the same hand and that one of them, M. Pritchard, supposedly a Baptist minister, was not in the Baptist handbook.[3] 'Ours is not an institution', Spurgeon insisted with some force, 'by which young men are enticed into the ministry; it is far more one that aims to keep out of the sacred office those who are not called to it. We are continually declining candidates because we question their fitness.' He added that some of those who were rejected had money and education, but these were not factors that were taken into account.[4] Selection of candidates was, as George Rogers put it, determined principally 'by evidences of eminent piety; of adaptation for public teaching; of great zeal for the salvation of souls, and of instances of actual usefulness'.[5] Usefulness included two years of preaching experience which had resulted in conversions.[6] In 1886 Spurgeon outlined a typical route that someone took into College. He pictured someone who had begun to speak in cottage meetings and in the open air. Soon the young preacher attracted attention, often gathering some young admirers. Then contact was established with the College. 'A young minister comes down from the Pastors' College', said Spurgeon, 'and preaches in such an admirable manner that our young hero enquires whence he came.' Such aspiring preachers would then write to Spurgeon. The main thing that the College was looking for was

The Pastors' College, Temple Street Building

not an impressive application. The spelling in the letter might, as it was read in the College, seem 'original', and the grammar 'heretical'. But if the applicant could convince Spurgeon that there was 'something in him' then he would be accepted.[7]

A number of students came to the College from outside London, including from some of the many village Baptist churches (in Spurgeon's descriptions, from 'Slocum-in-the-Marsh'), but more were already living in London. For many of these a way into study was through the College's evening classes.[8] The classes started in 1862, first in the Tabernacle and then in Temple Street, and covered 'the Classics, Mathematics, Natural Science, and all the branches of a liberal English education'. George Rogers and David Gracey were among the teachers, and other lecturers were recruited to teach such subjects as writing and elocution. About 150 students were attending.[9] W.R. Selway, a Congregational layman and a surveyor with the Metropolitan Board of Works, was a popular science lecturer, known for his 'interesting experiments'. He taught a remarkable range of subjects within the main College courses and the evening classes, including Anatomy, Geology, Astronomy, Mechanics, Electricity and Magnetism.[10] One student, Jacob Forth, described the struggle to be at the classes at the end of a working day, but also the benefit he gained from discussing topics.[11] Public lectures were held, featuring well-known preachers such as Joseph Parker and Newman Hall as well as specialists in other fields. E.B. Aveling, a Lecturer in Comparative Anatomy, spoke on 'The Biography of a Frog'.[12] Students from other denominations benefitted from the classes.[13] In the 1870s Spurgeon referred to the evening classes using terminology associated with the development in the 1850s of 'Working Men's Colleges', calling the College classes a 'Working Men's College of the Christian order'.[14] In this period the classes had 300 names on the books and an average attendance of 160.[15]

In the 1880s Spurgeon was more emphatic about the need for a broad and adequate education if ministry was going to be effective. In 1871 he had argued that the preacher's language 'must not be that of the classroom, but of all classes'.[16] A decade later, however, he suggested that 'to reach a generation in which education is becoming more general' God would select those who could communicate well.[17] By the later 1880s he was speaking, no doubt from experience, of young people trained under the national schooling system (in place from 1870) making fun of preachers who were 'vicious in pronunciation and faulty in grammar'.[18] The College course included general education, with an emphasis on mathematics, Latin, and science, and in 1881 science was upgraded when the College began to utilise F.R. Cheshire, a minister and lecturer at the South Kensington Science Museum. As an example of Cheshire's practical application of science, he acquired a 'portable magic-lantern' which was used by students in churches.[19] With the length of the College courses being extended to three or even four years, the evening classes as a basis for intensive College training became less relevant and numbers at these classes fell. Nonetheless, they continued into the 1890s, with a Pitman's shorthand class added to the main list of options. Members of the advanced classes were studying Latin and Greek texts, such as Caesar and Homer, and discussion and sermon classes were particularly popular.[20] In David Gracey's time as Principal those entering the College tended to have already had a basic education.[21] Gracey insisted that Spurgeon had seen, with 'instinctive wisdom', that society was moving away from elitism.[22]

Linked with Spurgeon's desire to open the College to those whose education was limited was his commitment to training those who could not contribute to the cost of such training. In 1870 a comparison was made between the approach of the Pastors' College, which sought to facilitate education for poor applicants, and that of other Colleges. Normally attendance at a College, Spurgeon noted, 'involved necessarily a considerable outlay to the student, for even where the education was free, books, clothes, and other incidental expenses required a considerable sum per annum'.[23] Because of the age of the students most had not had any opportunity to make any money of their own. Many were apprentices – for example in the grocery trade, the clothing trade, cabinet making, or printing. Others were farm-workers or shop assistants. A small number had been to University. By the 1880s the Pastors' College had supplied many students 'not only with tuition and books, gratis, but with board and lodging, and in some cases with clothes and pocket-money'. However, it was also the case by that stage that the numbers able to support themselves financially, either wholly or partly, had increased.[24] Some of the students in the 1880s had been working in commerce, in 'business houses', in government posts, or in solicitor's offices, and either they or their families could contribute to the costs of training. Spurgeon believed that this trend would continue.

Celebrating diversity

Alongside Spurgeon's concern for the disadvantaged, he had a vision of a diverse College community in which there would be different gifts. In 1870 he insisted that 'we want the profound and the eloquent of the first rank; we need also the earnest and godly of ordinary capacity'. He wanted some ministers who would be suited to Bethnal Green and others who would be at home in London's West End.[25] H.T. Spufford, a journalist living in Bexleyheath, Kent, who was a member of Trinity, Bexleyheath, was introduced in 1871 to Spurgeon by his minister. Discussion took place about whether Spufford would apply to the College. 'We want the best men of the day in the College', Spurgeon told Spufford during the meeting, 'are you one of them?' Soon after this Spufford was offered a post with a leading newspaper, but he decided to apply to enter the College. 'Come in a fortnight', Spurgeon commanded.[26] Four years later Spurgeon commented that he hoped to see more students coming to the College from the upper and middle classes. He believed that 'their early advantages would be much in their favour, and help them to take leading positions in the church'. He also thought that wealthy parents often discouraged their sons who wanted to preach the gospel.[27] Greater diversity in the ministry was a goal.

Mr and Mrs C.H.Richardson with Mr and Mrs T.L.Johnson

This included some ethnic diversity. In the 1860s and 1870s three Black students came from North America to the College: J.H. Magee, who came in 1867 from Toronto, Canada, and who went on to ministry in Nashville, Tennessee; T.L. Johnson, who had been a pastor in Denver, Colorado, came in 1875; and Calvin Richardson, from First Baptist Church, Washington, DC, came in 1877. Both Johnson and Richardson went on to undertake mission work in West Africa. A decade later Simeon Gordon came from the West Indies to the College and went as a missionary to the Congo. Thomas Johnson, who told his remarkable story in *Twenty-Eight Years a Slave*, contacted the American Baptist Union in Boston

Simeon Gordon

about his desire to go to Africa, and was also in touch with W. Hind Smith, of the YMCA, Peter Street, Manchester, who enabled him to come to England.[28] On his first day in the College, Johnson, who was aged forty and was very nervous about study, was given 'a very cordial welcome' by the students. Both staff and students gave Johnson extra help. Archibald Fergusson invited him to his home in Ealing for personal tuition. Johnson was, naturally, very keen to speak to Spurgeon, whose sermons he had read in America. Johnson wrote about meeting Spurgeon: 'His first words set me at ease, but his sympathetic kindness was beyond my highest hope. He took me by the hand, asked me a few questions, and wished me success…. I felt I had been talking to a dear loving friend. I at once fell in love with dear Mr. Spurgeon… I felt so happy in his presence, and so at home with him, that I could not help saying, "Well, thank God he is my friend."'[29] By the late twentieth century ethnic diversity was to be a notable feature of the College.

Diversity did not extend in Spurgeon's time to the training of women. Spurgeon did, however, show interest in women preachers. When Danzy Sheen, a Primitive Methodist, was a College student Spurgeon asked him what he thought of Miss Buck, a well-known Primitive Methodist preacher. Sheen had heard her preaching and gave Spurgeon an account of the sermon. Spurgeon expressed admiration for what he considered an intellectual discourse, describing this as 'masculine', but added that he did not think it was intellectual preaching that won most people to Christ.[30] Mary Clarissa Buck was a popular preacher and travelled vast distances taking special services. On occasions the crowds wanting to hear her meant that people had to be turned away.[31] Although Spurgeon did not approve of such female ministry, he did train 'Bible women' as local evangelists.[32] The question of training women came up at a College Committee in 1920. This was at a time when there was concern as to the best way to train women for the Baptist Union's Deaconess Order. It was agreed that the funds of the College were for training men for ministry, but there was consideration of 'what structural alterations would be requisite for the convenience of lady students'.[33] Presumably this had to do with installing female toilets. At that point the College was still non-residential. The needs of the Deaconesses were met through the use of Havelock Hall, Hampstead, as a Women's Training College for Deaconesses. The first woman to enter Baptist ministry, Edith Gates, qualified as a probationer Baptist minister in 1922, but (as we will see) the College did not accept its first female students until the 1960s and the number of women in Baptist ministry remained very small until the 1970s.

Finally, Spurgeon offered options to students and ministers which can be seen as early examples of open learning and continuing development. Not all the students who attended classes at the College were enrolled as full-time students. In 1881 it was noted that German students, presumably Baptists associated with Spurgeon's friend, Johann Oncken (who exercised a European-wide ministry from Hamburg), had attended classes during their vacations. Also members of other theological colleges were usually to be seen at lectures in the Pastors' College.[34] For pastors who were 'earnest, useful, plodding, but conscious of a great lack', the College offered the opportunity to gain knowledge and also, as Spurgeon put it, to 'cultivate the imagination'.[35] In some cases these ministers would come

Student group 1956-1960

to College for a year. In addition, Spurgeon hoped that the time that students spent in College would open up to them 'a world of reading and research' which they would explore throughout their ministry.[36] Spurgeon also saw the potential of his published *Lectures to my Students* in helping ministers unable to come to College. He commented in 1887: 'I have lately heard of a case in which a good country brother, who has never brushed his back against a college wall, was much assisted to quit his native roughness by his wife reading the Lectures to him, and pausing every now and then to say, "There, James, that's you."' If this happened more frequently, Spurgeon mused, it might not be necessary for such ministers to come to College.[37] Although this was an overstatement for the sake of effect, there is no doubt that Spurgeon was committed to training through a variety of methods.

Changing constituencies

The backgrounds and experiences of those entering the College in the twentieth century were in contrast with what had been the case in the nineteenth century. In 1948 Eric Worstead explained that two years of preaching was demanded of applicants to the College – a requirement that had remained unchanged - and that the College also required two years 'in business', which was seen as ensuring that those entering ministry had tested their faith and their ability to relate to others. Worstead explained that it was the duty of the College to equip students 'in the finest manner' so that they would be able to give a convincing reason for their faith when speaking to people outside the churches. Significantly, Worstead listed the groups to whom ministers might be speaking as teachers, doctors, scientists, university dons, and artisans.[38] The contrast with the earlier stress on 'the masses' was striking. In the 1950s and 1960s those entering College had worked as

College group 1907

technicians, teachers, nurses, solicitor's clerks, librarians, estate agents, surveyors, and police officers, or in office work, the engineering industry, retail and insurance. Stanley Dewhurst, surveying the range of experience of those entering College in 1961, noted that the average age of the new students was twenty-three. Of the sixteen new entrants (there were normally about 40 in the College), ten were from London and the South East.[39] The Spurgeon's constituency in this period reflected a predominantly southern English, middle-class Baptist world.

Along with this change came a greater emphasis on academic achievement. This was true under David Gracey, but at that time the College rejected 'arbitrary regulations' of 'secular' authorities.[40] Under McCaig, however, students began to take examinations at London University.[41] This reflected a trend in Baptist training. In 1870 only 1% of English Baptist ministers had been to a university. By 1901 the figure was 8%.[42] Most students, however, took internal College examinations. A focus on factual knowledge made it possible for some to gain high marks by memorising information. In 1910 McCaig, speaking of the encouraging examination results, highlighted one student with an average of 99% for all subjects.[43] The syllabus changed little, but in 1924 McCaig reported that he was now dealing with theories about the ultimate annihilation of the impenitent.[44] From the 1930s, the external BD degree of London University dominated the academic life of Spurgeon's. In 1936-7, Stanley Dewhurst and Eric Worstead, both later College tutors, gained first class honours degrees. Two decades on M.F. Williams, later a well known preacher in the denomination, was the first Spurgeon's student to receive a Baptist Union scholarship for further study, and three students in the 1950s subsequently went into academic life - A.A. Anderson, R.E. Clements and Paul Ballard. Anderson lectured in Old Testament at Edinburgh and Manchester Universities. Clements, who acknowledged his debt to George Beasley-Murray, had two pastoral ministries and then a distinguished lecturing career at Edinburgh, Cambridge, and as Old Testament Professor, King's College London. Ballard's lectureships in Wales led to a chair in Religious and Theological Studies, Cardiff University. The College appeared to have a growing academic contribution to make.[45] By this stage it was thought desirable to have two 'A' levels to enter Spurgeon's. Many students received local education grants. Talks took place about affiliation with London University, but this was not feasible as students at final BD stage would have been virtually full-time at King's College London.[46]

College Faculty 1990-1991
Standing left to right: Paul Beasley-Murray (Principal), Bob Archer, Colin Brown, Stuart Christine, Alastair Campbell, Brian Stanley, Mike Nicholls. Seated left to right: Nigel Wright, Debra Reid, Martin Selman

The College Council, which was responsible for the selection of those who entered College, was determined, however, that the interest in academic achievement did not overwhelm the concern for other – more fundamental - aspects of College training. In 1963 the College Council reiterated that those who entered the College had to have 'personal experience of Christ as Saviour and Lord, and a desire to bear witness to him', membership in a Baptist church, conviction of a call, blessing upon their preaching, and readiness to accept the discipline of four years of study.[47] In the mid-1960s, when over sixty students were in training in the College (the highest number up to that point in the century), about a quarter of those entering College had already been assistant pastors. Where it was felt that applicants lacked experience, pre-collegiate, one-year student assistantships were arranged. The concern within the faculty, too, was that products of Spurgeon's should be good, all-round ministers. George Beasley-Murray, as J.J. Brown put it, 'combined the mind of a scholar with the heart of an evangelist'.[48] He wished the students to be effective in practical ministry, and since he and his full–time colleagues – Geoffrey Rusling, Frank Fitzsimmonds and Stanley Dewhurst, with Rex Mason and Lewis Drummond added later - could not cover all areas of practical ministerial training, lecturers came in to deal with pastoral work, hospital ministry, Sunday school work and psychology.

It was from the 1970s that the College community began to change significantly. Students came from a wider range of backgrounds. In 1959 only two students were married but by the end of the 1970s most were married. The average age by the 1980s was early thirties. The College expanded considerably, with new CNAA courses being offered, and the teaching team also expanded. From the 1990s the College offered University of Wales awards. In 1980 the academic staff comprised Raymond Brown as Principal, Frank Fitzsimmonds as Vice-Principal, and John Maile, Peter Manson, Bruce Milne, Mike Nicholls, Martin Selman and Brian Stanley as tutors. Robert Thompson, formerly Principal of the New Zealand Baptist Theological College, joined later when Milne moved to Canada. During Paul Beasley-Murray's principalship the faculty increased by one third, to eleven: the first female faculty member, Debra Reid, was appointed, and other significant appointments included Colin Brown and Arthur Rowe (both higher education teachers), Stuart Christine, and (initially as research fellow) Alastair Campbell, who had trained at Regent's Park College and was a pastor in Northampton. Under Michael Quicke and then Nigel Wright, the tutors were: Martin Selman, Debra Reid and Joy Osgood in Old Testament, with Martin Selman also serving as Deputy Principal; Alastair Campbell and Arthur Rowe, followed by Pieter Lalleman and Calvin Samuel in New Testament; Colin Brown and John Colwell in Christian Doctrine and Ethics; Peter Stevenson in Applied Theology; Ian Randall in Church History and Spirituality; and Bob Archer, Bill Allen and Stuart Murray, and later Chris Voke and Rachel Dutton, in pastoral and/or mission studies. A sociologist, Keith White, was a long-term associate lecturer. Steve Holmes was a research fellow.[49] Tutors were drawn from a wide constituency, with Joy Osgood the first ordained Anglican minister to become a tutor, and Calvin Samuel, a Methodist minister, the first Black member of the teaching staff.

Opportunities for women

The number of women training for Baptist ministry increased, albeit slowly, from the 1960s, when Margaret Jarman became the first Spurgeon's woman student. She had trained in the 1950s for the Deaconess Order and had served churches at Pontesbury, Lord's Hill and Brockton in Shropshire, from 1956 to 1961. Many Deaconesses, although not ordained, were in essence serving as ministers. Margaret Jarman had a Diploma in Theology and was given two years leave of absence from ministry to complete the BD. In 1962 she reflected on her initial experiences at Spurgeon's. In her braver moments before coming she had asked why the privilege of studying at Spurgeon's should be confined to men but in more timid mood she had trembled at the prospect of being the only woman student among sixty men. 'I had coped with three churches for the past five years', she mused, 'and I had dealt with such things as tractors and cows, and even bulls – but dare I undertake this new hazard?!' It was not long before she felt herself part of Spurgeon's. There were one or two problems: 'Will men – er – I mean 'students', please… 'Brethren – oh – er – and sister…'. But Margaret Jarman spoke of the value of the training, teaching, discussion, study and worship. 'Here', she said, 'is the opportunity to think together about the implications and application of the Gospel to our work in the churches.'[50]

In accepting Margaret Jarman as a student the College Council made the point that the College was not committed 'to any particular view concerning the training of women for ministry'.[51] However, the trend was towards recognising women as ministers. A second woman, Gladys

Group of Church -based students at Graduation with Rev. Chris Voke in 2000

Seymour (later Smith), became a student in 1962. She had served with the BMS in China and India. Margaret Jarman became the Organising Secretary of the Baptist Union Deaconess Department and in 1987 was the first woman minister to be President of the Baptist Union. She was also the first chair of the Baptist Union Retreat Group, formed in 1988. Gladys Seymour completed her BD in 1964. The Minutes of the Council of 13 October 1964 read: 'Leaving men set an all-time record in failures; all who attempted Diploma and B.D. final examinations failed; Miss Seymour alone gained B.D. This has been a blot on the name of the College which it will be difficult to erase.' It seemed that the men had spent too much time on activities outside the College.[52] Gladys Seymour was ordained in 1966 and took up ministry at Markyate Baptist Church, Herts. These first two women students of the College were referred to in the *College Record* in 1967 as 'exceptional women of whom the denomination and the College are proud'.[53] Despite this, there were still references to 'men' leaving the College to take up ministry. In 1965 the College was approached to see if it might be willing to receive candidates for the Deaconess Order. The College was willing to explore possibilities.[54] In the event the Deaconess Order was brought to an end, with the Deaconesses accepting that their function had become ministerial.[55]

During the 1970s and 1980s a number of women students trained at the College, although several of them were not seeking ordination. In 1972, for example, two women were accepted for training, Susan Melville, who wished 'to equip herself more effectively for church work and addressing meetings', and Kathryn Foster (later Hewitt), who wished to became a Religious Education teacher. They were joined in 1973 by Joan Maple, a school teacher and deacon at Greenford Baptist Church who wished to obtain a BD and continue teaching. After one year of study Susan Melville was accepted for ministerial training.[56] She settled in Dagenham and later entered the Methodist ministry. In the 1980s a number of women studied part-time at the College in order to equip themselves for work as team members in local churches, without being ordained. During the Pastoral Studies fourth year, under the direction of Peter Manson, a number of wives of students took courses. Other women entered ordained ministry. Nancy Hill settled in 1981 at Baxter Gate, Loughborough, as a supplementary (non-stipendiary) minister. Helen Matthews settled in

1984 at Waterlooville, and after other local church ministries moved to the BMS in 1990. In 1992 Anne-Wilkinson Hayes, who had studied at the College from 1983 to 1987 and had then been associate minister at Manvers Street, Bath, joined the staff of the Baptist Union and exercised a significant influence as Secretary for social affairs. She was later appointed to a regional ministerial post in Australia. Ruth Gouldbourne, who studied for a year at Spurgeon's, became tutor in church history at Bristol Baptist College, and has written on women in Baptist ministry.[57]

In 1990 representatives of the Baptist Colleges meeting together issued a statement of intent regarding women in ministry. This recognised that patterns of training for ministry had been inadequately supportive of women training for Christian ministry and made a commitment to providing a supportive environment for ministerial formation that would be free from discrimination. The Colleges agreed to promote and encourage the ministry of women in the churches. At the Spurgeon's College Council in October 1990 Nigel Wright introduced the statement and suggested that the Council accept it and give it publicity. The Council agreed, and decided to set up a working group to consider the outworking of the proposals.[58] Although some women students, such as Sally Nelson, trained through the College-based course, the College's church-based courses provided a helpful route into ordained ministry for a number of women in the 1990s, among them Julie Shimizu, Lisa Holmes, Helen Wordsworth, Kate Coleman, Juliet Kilpin, Sheila Martin and Gill Lee. Several of these became known in wider Baptist life. Dotha Blackwood became a lecturer at Moorlands College, near Bournemouth. On occasions married couples trained together and both entered Baptist ministry, for example Paul and Lynda Henstock, who trained in the 1970s, and Steve and Jan Worthy in the 1990s. In 2000, of the twenty-nine leaving students seven were women who would enter Baptist ministry – Julie Aylward, Carol Bostridge, Jayne Durham, Gill Hawkins, Amanda James, Freddie Latham-Durrant and Karen Stallard. Although such a high proportion was unusual, it did indicate that at a time when women still constituted under 7% of Baptist ministers, the College was providing women with opportunities to fulfil their calling.

Resourcing ministries

Although the College saw considerable change from the 1960s, the primary focus of the College remained the same – to give opportunities to people to train for ministry. From the 1980s Roy Slack, Director of the extension department, was involved in publicity, College roadshows and liaising with churches seeking student preachers on Sundays. In the 1990s the College had Directors of Communication - Clive Doubleday, whose wife Ruth had also been a (part-time) student, and later Brian Curtis. Paul Beasley-Murray organised days to discover about ministry (Minfax days) which could attract up to 150 people. While the Baptist Union investigated both shortages and over-supply of ministers (at different times), the consistent concern at Spurgeon's was to develop ministries. From the 1970s many new team ministries in Baptist churches opened up new opportunities. Among those trained at the College who undertook pastoral ministries that had wider influence from the 1970s to the 1990s were: Peter Goodlad, in Ilford and Northampton; Douglas Hollidge at the Metropolitan Tabernacle and in Forest Gate; Peter Pearmain in New Milton; Brian Butcher in Banbury; Ben Davies in Bracknell; Mike Wood at Lewin Road, Streatham; David Beer, in Tonbridge and Frinton-on-Sea; Roger Martin, in Poynton, Leigh-on-Sea, and then Stockton-on-Tees; Alan Pain in Sutton Coldfield; Andrew Kane at Durrington and Woking; Robert Amess at Duke Street, Richmond; Derek Hills in New Malden and Tonbridge; Steve Ibbotson in Leeds; Steve Gaukroger at Stopsley, Luton, and Gold Hill; and Andrew Rigden Green, at Upton Vale, Torquay. Most of these churches – some of which were among the largest in the denomination (with over 500 people) – developed team ministries.

Even larger Black-majority Baptist churches were to be found by the 1990s. When Kingsley Appiagyei came from Ghana to study at Spurgeon's in the late 1980s a group of eight people began to meet in his flat. By 1991 this was a Ghanaian Baptist Fellowship of 180, in West Norwood, London. A year later, when this congregation applied to join the Union, there were 350 worshippers, 95% Ghanaian.[59] Another predominantly Ghanaian congregation was Calvary Charismatic Baptist Church, which began in 1994 under the leadership of Francis Sarpong, a College student. It had almost 400 members two years later.[60] Both these congregations grew to over 1,000. Among other Black and Asian ministers who trained at Spurgeon's and became involved in various multi-cultural ministries in Britain were: Fred George, at East Barnet - Union President in 1997; Rupert Lazar in West Croydon; Chris Andre-Watson, at Kenyon, Brixton, and then a BMS regional representative; Wale Hudson-Roberts, at Stroud Green, London, and then Racial Justice Co-ordinator for the Union; Ram Gidoomal, businessman, church leader and politician; Kate Coleman, at Chalk Farm in London, and then in Birmingham; Phyllis Manners, in Peckham; and Kumar Rajagopalan, in Wood Green and then on the LBA regional team. 'Black Light' courses introduced issues connected with Black theology. By 2004 the percentage of those entering College (all students, not only full-timers) who were from minority ethnic backgrounds was about 25%, reflecting the way in which the College was equipping Baptists and others from across the churches of London and elsewhere within multi-cultural Britain. Kingsley Appiagyei said in 2001 that he saw himself as a missionary seeking to strengthen the church in the UK.[61]

The College supported continuing ministries in a variety of ways in the decades after the Second World War. Several Spurgeon's-trained ministers became Superintendents from the 1950s to the 1980s - Harold Tebbitt and David Harper (Eastern Area), Douglas Sparkes and Arthur Thompson (London) and Peter Tongeman (South Eastern). Tebbitt, Harper and Thompson all contributed significantly to the College through chairing College Council. Douglas Sparkes became Union Deputy General Secretary, Geoffrey Rusling became

Bev Thomas

Union Head of Ministry, and Ernest Clipsham also served the Union. Eric Watson became General Superintendent of the Baptist Union of Scotland (BUS) and Andrew Rollinson the BUS Ministry Adviser. Some from Spurgeon's became College Principals - David Kingdon at the Irish Baptist College, Peter Cotterell at London Bible College, and Richard Kidd at Northern College. Within Spurgeon's, an MTh in Applied Theology and later an MTh in Preaching (the first in Britain) in partnership with the ecumenical College of Preachers, offered development opportunities. John Colwell, who had trained at the College in the 1970s and then had pastorates in Maldon and Catford, shaped the MTh in Applied Theology. Peter Stevenson then became course director.

MTh courses attracted participants from a range of ministries. In the first ten years over 200 enrolled in the Applied Theology MTh. Post-collegiate conferences were held, and Nigel Wright initiated training at College – one day a month - entitled 'Centre for Continuing Development in Ministry', led by Colin Buckland (a student in the 1970s) of the Claybury Trust. A number of ministers also undertook - especially from the 1990s – research for MPhil and PhD degrees, and most recently for a Doctor of Ministry.

A further resource giving opportunities for study at all levels has been the College library. There has been a library at the College since its beginnings. In its early period the Library was housed in a room at the Metropolitan Tabernacle. As books were difficult to come by, a circulating library was in operation. Books were packed in boxes and sent round to former students, many of whom were serving in churches in isolated parts of the country. These were kept for two months and then despatched to the next address on the list. As many as thirty-four boxes could be in circulation at any one time. When the Temple Street premises opened, the library was moved to an octagon room on the top floor, known as 'The Upper Room', where it served the students for many years. When the College moved to South Norwood Hill the library was scattered in various rooms throughout the building. In 1937 an annexe, designed to match the original building, was built at a cost of £4,000 so that the library's entire stock could be housed in one room. Following the death of Percy Evans, an appeal was set up to enlarge sections of the library. In the 1950s there were 12,000 volumes, but this was to grow to a first class academic library of 50,000 volumes. In 1977 New College, London, closed, and several thousand theological books from there came to Spurgeon's. By the early 1980s the library had run out of space and the students' games room was converted to form the current Reference Library. Brian Stanley devoted part of his time to the library in this period, but in 1985 a professional librarian, Judy Powles, was appointed. In 1990 a computer system was introduced to replace the card catalogues and later an automated self-issue system was added.[62] Opportunities for study were being extended.

Conclusion

C.H. Spurgeon was determined to draw into the orbit of theological training many who felt shut out. Although the College achieved a very great deal, he felt more could be done. In 1865 he noted that many suitable applicants had been declined, presumably because of limitations of space or finance, 'which shows', he insisted, that much of 'the kind of evangelistic and pastoral agency which the present age requires' was being lost.[63] In the early years Spurgeon gave great attention to opening up educational opportunities. He realised that as standards of education increased the need for ministers to be educated and well trained was pressing. He spoke of 'a great educational advance among all classes', and argued that even in country villages, where, according to tradition, 'nobody knows nothing', schoolteachers were making a difference.[64] As the College developed, it became a diverse community. People of different abilities trained together. Training to support continuing ministry was developed in new ways. Lay training opportunities also increased, especially from the 1970s. Evening classes were re-introduced in the 1970s,[65] then one day a week courses were added, and in the 1980s Paul Beasley-Murray launched popular lay leadership weekends and summer schools. Changes took place in the 1990s, with DELTA courses offered in local churches. In the later twentieth century diversity within the College increased: women became part of the student community and significant ethnic diversity was evident. A Diversity and Equal Opportunities Working Group was formed, which included Bev Thomas, a College governor active in this field, Black and Asian ministers trained at Spurgeon's, and representatives of the College staff and students. Within the field of equal opportunities, Roy Slack took on the role of disability officer. Although many changes can be identified, the original desire of the College to serve the churches remained unchanged. As Spurgeon put it in 1882: 'To build a meeting house, to found a school, to commence a village mission, to scatter pure literature – all these are admirable; but in equipping a pastor you have set in place the motive power which will effect those and a thousand other grand designs.'[66]

1   *AP*, 1890-91, p. 3.

2   *S and T*, June 1881, p. 302.

3   Murray, ed., *Letters of Charles Haddon Spurgeon* (Edinburgh: Banner of Truth, 1992), p. 118.

4   *AP*, 1886-87, p. 4.

5   Rogers, 'Outline', in *Outline* (1867), p. 11.

6   *S and T*, April 1867, p. 181.

7   *AP*, 1885-86, pp. 22-4.

8   *S and T*, April 1870, p. 149

9   'The Evening Classes', *Outline* (1867), pp. 30-7; *Outline*, 1868, p. 4.

10 *S and T*, April 1870, p. 150.

11 'The Evening Classes', pp. 37-8.

12 *S and T*, September 1878, p. 465.

13 *S and T*, February 1873, p. 90.

14 *S and T*, November 1876, p. 528.

15 *S and T*, August 1878, p. 417.

16 *S and T*, April, 1871, pp. 217-18; cf. AP, 1870, pp. 5-6.

17 *S and T*, May 1882, p. 259

18 *AP*, 1886-87, p. 4.

19 Bebbington, 'Spurgeon and British Evangelical Theological Education', pp. 229-30.

20 *AP*, 1894-95, pp. 7-8; *AP*, 1898-99, p. 11.

21 Bebbington, Spurgeon and British Evangelical Theological Education', pp. 233-4.

22 *S and T*, June 1892, p. 278.

23 *S and T*, April 1870, pp. 145-6.

24 *S and T*, June 1881, p. 302.

25 *AP*, 1870, p. 10.

26 *S and T*, December 1901, p. 615.

27 *S and T*, February 1875, pp. 91-2.

28 Johnson, *Twenty-Eight Years a Slave*, pp. 78-80.

29 Ibid, pp. 88-9.

30 Sheen, *Pastor C.H. Spurgeon*, p. 80.

31 E.D. Graham, 'Chosen by God: The Female Travelling Preachers of Early Primitive Methodism', in T. Macquiban, ed., *Methodism in its Cultural Milieu*, Westminster Wesley Series, No. 2 (Cambridge: Applied Theology Press, 1994), pp. 85-98.

32 *S and T*, January 1865, p. 31.

33 Minutes of the College Committee, 25 March 1920 (Minute Book 1898-1930, Box 6).

34 *S and T*, June 1881, p. 302.

35 *S and T*, May 1887, p. 206.

36 *AP*, 1885-86, p. 26.

37 *S and T*, May 1887, p. 210.

38 *College Record*, August 1948, pp. 5-7.

39 *College Record*, December 1961, pp. 18-19.

40 *AP*, 1886-87, p. 12.

41 *AP*, 1895-96, pp. 9-10.

42 J.E.B. Munson, 'The Education of Baptist Ministers, 1870-1900', *BQ*, Vol. 26, No. 7 (1976), p. 321.

43 *AP*, 1909-10, p. 9.

44 *AP*, 1923-24, p. 6.

45 Minutes of the College Executive Committee, 5 October 1956.

46 Minutes of the College Executive Committee and the Council, 9 June 1959.

47 *College Record*, June 1963, pp. 14-15,

48 *College Record*, December 1973, p. 11.

49 He then took up a post at King's College London, and later at St Andrew's University.

50 *College Record*, June 1962, pp. 9-10.

51 Minutes of College Council, 9 December 1960.

52 Minutes of College Council, 13 October 1964.

53 *College Record*, December 1967, pp. 39-40.

54 Minutes of College Council, 19 February 1965.

55 N. Morris, *Sisters of the People: The Order of Baptist Deaconesses, 1890-1975* (Bristol: University of Bristol, 2002), p. 32; Deaconess Committee Minutes, 17 September 1974; 23 January 1975; Minutes of the Baptist Union Council, 11 and 12 March 1975.

56 Minutes of College Council, 21 March 1973.

57 R.M.B. Gouldbourne, *Reinventing the Wheel: Women and ministry in English Baptist life* (Oxford: Whitley Publns., 1997).

58 The statement was received by the College Council on 31 October 1990 and is held with the minutes.

59 *BT*, 11 March 1991, p. 11. K. Appiagyei, 'Reaching Africans in London: An Ethnic Ministry', *The Baptist Ministers' Journal*, Vol. 238 (April 1992), pp. 6-10.

60 *BT*, 20 June 1996, p. 1.

61 *College Record*, April 2001, p. 3.

62 I am grateful to Judy Powles and to Raymond Brown for the information in this paragraph.

63 *S and T*, October 1865, p. 462.

64 Spurgeon, *All-Round Ministry*, p. 42.

65 These were part of the Extra-Mural services of the University of London.

66 *S and T*, May 1882, p. 260.

Chapter 7: Crossing continents

When the College began, none of those involved imagined that it would become an internationally-known institution. The needs in London and other parts of Britain were considered to be so great that it was appropriate for all the energies of those trained at the College to be directed towards meeting those needs. In addition, C.H. Spurgeon had doubts about the way in which some missionary societies, including the BMS, were operating. In 1858 he expressed his sympathy with the philosophy of George Muller, in Bristol, who never asked for money for his orphanage work but relied on prayer.[1] In 1863, when the BMS was in financial difficulties, it tried to enlist Spurgeon's help, but at that stage he did not wish to be associated with the Society, bluntly stating that his 'Utopian and spiritual' views of mission were at odds with the Society's stance. Later he reiterated his belief that mission activities should be 'in the highest degree works of faith', rather than based on fund-raising, and he also argued that the BMS had become an 'interposing medium' between the churches and the missionaries. He wanted churches and missionaries to be 'bound together by ties of mutual relation unknown at the present time'.[2] By 1866 the BMS had made some alterations to its constitution and Spurgeon's attitude began to change. The extent of the change is seen in the fact that in 1886 he said the Society was welcome to come to College Conference and 'look out some more heroes' for missionary work.[3] Brian Stanley, while a tutor at the College, undertook to write the official history of the BMS and in 1992 his definitive work, *The History of the Baptist Missionary Society, 1792-1992*, was published. Former College students have become involved in pioneering mission in a number of countries, not only with the BMS, while others have gone abroad to become ministers of existing churches, and still others have crossed continents to study at the College.

Early international links

In the early 1860s a number of students began to go overseas at the end of their College training. Crossing the Atlantic was to prove particularly popular, and among the first students going overseas were two – J. Turner and T. Harley – who went to Newfoundland and New Brunswick respectively. Another area which was to attract many students from the College was Australasia. In 1863 Frederick Hibberd, the first student to go to Australia, went to Hobart, Tasmania, and later had ministries in Sydney, playing a leading role in the formation of the Baptist Union of New South Wales. A wealthy couple in Tasmania, William and Mary Ann Gibson, who were devotees of Spurgeon's sermons, built fifteen churches from 1862, mostly Tabernacles, and invited products of the College to serve as ministers. By 1885 every church in Tasmania had as its pastor someone from the College.[4] Links with other parts of the world were established, for example with St Helena. It was reported in

Jamestown, St Helena

1867 that W.J. Cother, who had come to the College from Banbury in 1864, and had then gone to St Helena, had 'already seen a great revival of religion upon the rock'. In a period of less than nine months fifty-eight people, who were described as 'chiefly converts through our brother's ministry', had been accepted for baptism by the church.[5] Cother moved to Australia and then returned to St Helena where he remained until 1884. The church built up to a peak of 205 members but then declined to 118 due to emigration.[6]

The international dimension of the College's ministry grew. By the later 1860s Spurgeon was seeing this as a crucial element in the fulfilment of his vision for training effective pastors. Thomas Ness, who settled at the East London Tabernacle, Stepney, in 1865, had to resign because of ill health, and moved to Melbourne in 1868, where he began to train potential ministers. Spurgeon sent £100 to help with the training and wrote of what was happening as a branch of the Pastors' College. 'We welcome with joy', he said, 'the founding of a College in Melbourne, Australia, by our dear brother Mr. Ness, as the descendent of our own.'[7] This joy was somewhat premature, since Ness left Melbourne (returning to England in 1874) and the work did not continue. However, the episode gives a good indication of the way in which Spurgeon's thinking was developing. By 1873 *The Sword and the Trowel* was reporting on twenty-one former students of the College in ministry in America and seven in parts Australia.[8] In the case of most of these, their first ministry after College was in Britain, and this led to an invitation to go abroad. On many occasions the choice of a minister was left by churches overseas to Spurgeon's discretion.[9] Others pioneered new churches. Mark Noble went to Nebraska, USA, in 1868

Toowomba Baptist Church, Queensland

and began farming to make a living. He gathered a church through people whom he met.[10] The international links also attracted students from other countries. The first Black student to come to College, J.H. Magee, became Principal in 1869 of the Baptist College in Nashville, Tennessee, and later moved to ministry in a large church in Ohio.

Following the reconciliation of Spurgeon with the BMS in 1866, the call to overseas mission became more prominent in the life of the College. E.B. Underhill, the Secretary of the BMS, was invited in 1866 to lecture in the College on the Society.[11] Three years later Isaac Pegg, from Willenhall, who came to the College in 1867, went to the Bahamas. By

1873 he was working in St. Domingo under the direction of Underhill, and had gathered so many people that he returned to Britain to raise money to build a large chapel. In March 1873 Spurgeon featured a long report by Pegg, describing growth in St. Domingo and opportunities in Porto Rico. Spurgeon added a note to say that Pegg had 'become one of the ablest missionaries we have ever met with', and that his 'tact, ability, and grace' were beyond praise. Pegg's appeal for money was given full backing by Spurgeon, who took the opportunity to say that he had often prayed that the College would become 'the mother of missionaries'.[12] A month later Spurgeon called Pegg an 'apostle'.[13] R.E. Gammon was also with the BMS in the West Indies and saw considerable numbers of people baptised.[14] J.J. Kendon, from Providence Chapel, Goudhurst, Kent, studied at the College in the 1870s and then went to Jamaica. In 1882 he reported that between January and April he had baptised fifty-eight people and was pastoring a church of 850 members.[15] By the mid-1870s one former student, F. Groombridge, had gone to China with the China Inland Mission (CIM), and two others, J.P. Wigston and Thomas Blamire (both from Congregational churches - in Penrith and Carlisle respectively), had gone to Spain. Spurgeon hoped for a 'noble army' and a 'numerous band' of missionaries going from the College.[16]

Multiplying ministers abroad

The more obvious development in the 1880s was the small army of those from the College going to pastorates overseas. In 1881 Spurgeon featured letters and news from pastors who were abroad, particularly those in Australia and North America. Thomas Spurgeon went to Australia in 1877, at the age of twenty-two, for the sake of his health, and found that the name of his father had great effect. Speaking in Melbourne in 1878, he quoted a letter from C.H. Spurgeon and remarked that his hearers were delighted and 'sat forward in their seats to listen eagerly, as they always do when the magic name is pronounced'.[17] In introducing a letter from the College-trained ministers in Australia, Spurgeon commented on the 'very considerable number' of them to be found in Australia and New Zealand. 'I cannot forget', he said, 'that there I have a beloved son; but next to that in nearness to my heart is the fact that so many of my spiritual sons are there, prospering and bringing glory to God.' Spurgeon was clearly delighted to hear from them.[18] In the following year Thomas Spurgeon moved to New Zealand. The first student from the College to go to New Zealand, Charles Dallaston, in 1877, saw significant growth. In the same period Thomas Spurgeon established himself as the enormously popular pastor of the Auckland Tabernacle, which became the largest church in Australasia. A new building was built, modelled on the Metropolitan Tabernacle, London, to seat 1,200, and crowds of up to 1,500 attended. The College supplied significant numbers of ministers to the Baptist Union of New Zealand, from its foundation in 1882, and Thomas Spurgeon played a leading role in the Union.[19]

The letter to C.H. Spurgeon from the Australian pastors, dated 2 November 1880 and written from Melbourne, conveyed the sense of strong attachment that former students, not least those overseas, felt towards the College. They wrote that 'we can say that instead of distance or even time causing any abatement of love towards you personally, or towards the institution which we may with truth style our *Alma Mater*, we find it intensified and hallowed.' The meetings of the Victoria Baptist Association had brought ministers together, and they had been joined by Harry Woods from South Australia, and J.S. Harrison from Tasmania. This deeply personal letter spoke of the ministers having 'caught the spirit of burning love to souls' which characterised Spurgeon himself, and expressed to Spurgeon the hope that they would show the benefit through their ministries in Australia of 'all your care and that of the tutors and friends of the Tabernacle'. It was signed by W.C. Bunning from Geelong, William Clark from Ballarat, Alfred J. Clarke, who had worked as an evangelist with Manton Smith and was now in Melbourne, H.H. Garrett from Brighton, Henry Marsden from Kew, J.S. Harrison from Tasmania, Harry Woods from South Australia, and F.G. Buckingham from Melbourne.[20] Among those who went to Australia a little later was William Higlett, and in visiting groups of German Baptists in Queensland he discovered a large portrait of Spurgeon in nearly every home. In the first ninety years of the College's life, 106 ministers trained there went to Australia and New Zealand.[21]

Similar sentiments came from Canada and the USA. A letter of 6 April 1881 from Ontario, Canada, was addressed to Spurgeon and to the College Conference. James Spurgeon, during a recent visit to Canada, had formed a branch of the College Conference there. This letter spoke of the love that the ministers had for Spurgeon, and recalled occasions of prayer in the College when they heard Spurgeon 'sigh and groan his longings' for their future ministries. The ministers in Canada were, they said, 'in some cases separated even here by many dreary miles of continent', but they echoed the motto of the College – 'we still hold and are held to and by the old-time kindness; and, better still, "the form of sound words".' This was signed by Joseph Forth (a member of the Metropolitan Tabernacle and a College student in the 1860s), as President of the Canadian branch of the 'College Brotherhood'.[22] The Canadian branch continued to keep in touch with the College Conference. Those who went to the USA did not forge such strong bonds with each other. Spurgeon encouraged students to consider ministry in the USA, commenting in 1873 that in America a pastor was not 'starved down to the lowest living point, but is liberally supported.' He also noted, however, that some students who had been deemed unsuitable for ministry and dismissed from the College were 'said to be acceptable across the sea'.[23] Writing in the mid-twentieth century, at which point there were relatively few Spurgeon's-trained ministers in the USA, Robert Hughes recalled that in his ministry there in the 1890s, the College had been represented by fifty ministers, including C.A. Cook, in Bloomfield, New Jersey, William Willis in Boston, G.C. Williams in Mt. Vernon, Ohio, and P.J. Ward in Toledo, Ohio.[24] Not all who went to the USA stayed. Frank Dann's health broke down due to the extremes of climate in Minnesota, and in 1889 he returned to England.[25]

During the first half of the twentieth century the range of countries to which students

Falkland Islands Tabernacle.

went increased. The College had association with the Falkland Islands, where G.H. Harris worked before moving to Guernsey in 1890.[26] The small Baptist Chapel which was built on the Falklands in 1899 was named The Tabernacle. Some of the former students serving in other countries became internationally known figures, such as F.W. Boreham, who was considered to have been the last student Spurgeon accepted into the College before his death. Boreham's first ministry began in Mosgiel, New Zealand, in 1895, and was followed by pastorates in Hobart, Tasmania, and Armadale, a suburb of Melbourne. Boreham wrote over forty books, perhaps most notably *A Bunch of Everlastings* (1920).[27] E.A. Carter's Pioneer Mission extended its activities into France, into Holland, where Pastor Weenink of Stadskanaal was conducting missions, into areas of Europe where there were German Baptists, and into Russia.[28] An outstanding former

student who served in Russia and Latvia in the early twentieth century was William Fetler (known also as Basil Malof), a Latvian who studied at the College from 1903 to 1907. He addressed the Metropolitan Tabernacle Sunday School the day after his arrival at College, with Mr Neuf interpreting.[29] Fetler was supported by the Pioneer Mission and he saw remarkable results in St Petersburg, Moscow, and Riga, the capital of Latvia. As a result of his work in

Student group 1903-1907

St Petersburg a church building was opened in 1911 seating 2,000 people (Archibald McCaig attended the opening), and in 1927 a similar sized building, the Salvation Temple

Salvation Temple Riga

Revival Baptist Church, was opened in Riga. By this stage Fetler's own Russian Missionary Society had two hundred staff.[30] McCaig and Fetler edited a monthly magazine, *The Friend of Missions*.

World mission challenges

Spurgeon's hope in 1873 for many missionaries to go out from the College was to be fulfilled in the decades that followed. By the late 1870s students

had gone to such places as China, Japan, India, Italy and Spain.[31] There was great interest in this period in the CIM (later the Overseas Missionary Fellowship) which was started in 1865 by Hudson Taylor and became the largest Protestant mission in the world. From the mid-1870s a steady stream of people who had trained at the College or who belonged to the Metropolitan Tabernacle joined the CIM. Among the CIM's principles were interdenominationalism, the expectation that missionaries would wear Chinese dress and identify with the local people, and the conviction that all funds were to be raised 'by faith' rather than through appeals for money. Spurgeon enjoyed Taylor's company and admired his radical methods.[32] J.J. Turner, who was with the CIM, was a valued speaker at College Conferences and greetings were conveyed to Conference from those trained at the College who were working with the CIM. The College's connection with Japan was much more limited, but reports in 1879 from W.J. White in Japan spoke of 1,000 people wanting to be baptised.[33] India would attract a number of students, especially from the 1880s onwards. Within Europe, the College's early links with Spain were followed in the twentieth century by an interest in a former student, Frank Buffard, who was sent out from the East London Tabernacle in 1950 and served with the Spanish Gospel Mission.[34] H.H. Pullen served from 1898 with the Spezia Mission in Italy, founded in 1870.[35]

A determined effort was made in the 1880s and 1890s to broaden the minds of the students regarding world mission. J. Gelson Gregson, a BMS missionary who also travelled widely on behalf of the Keswick Convention movement, addressed the College Conference in 1880 and appealed for missionaries to go to India.[36] This was before Keswick itself allowed missionary appeals to take place. Gregson was regarded by some Keswick leaders as somewhat controversial in his advocacy of 'the baptism of the Spirit' for spiritual empowering.[37] A pan-denominational Missionary Association, of which the College was a part, convened well-attended meetings in London in this period. At a meeting in 1883, David Gracey chaired and E.E. Jenkins, the Secretary of the Wesleyan Missionary Society, delivered what was described as 'an eloquent and instructive address'. Jenkins spoke for a remarkable one and three quarter hours about new developments in Japan, India and China, and the report of the meeting stated that 'the students listened to him with the closest attention'.[38] Spurgeon also took students from the College to visit the East London Institute, Harley House, led by Grattan Guinness, who founded the Regions Beyond Missionary Union (RBMU), although there is some evidence that Spurgeon had reservations about Guinness' willingness to accept anyone who applied to the Institute for training.[39] In 1881 Spurgeon, drawing from the thinking of American Baptist missionary pioneer, Adoniram Judson, wished 'to make the Pastors' College a seed-garden for the church and for the world'.[40]

Although the College introduced students to a wide range of missionary activity from the 1880s onwards, Spurgeon wanted the College to have closer contact with missionaries than was sometimes possible through missionary societies. N. Hardingham Patrick, who had entered the College in 1886 and was a student pastor at St Mary Cray, was taken on in 1889 by the newly-formed Pastors' College Missionary Association, which undertook to provide his financial support.[41] Spurgeon wrote to Patrick: 'I rejoice that the way is cleared for your going to North Africa. As a brother looking to our own funds for support you are the first representative of the Foreign Mission of the College, and I am the more earnest that you should lead the way gloriously.' He continued: 'Aspire to be another "Patrick", - the apostle of North Africa, as he was of Ireland.'[42] The work undertaken by Patrick and his wife, based in Morocco and linked with the North Africa Mission, was initially discouraging. In the College's 1891-92 *Annual Report* he said that the preaching and the medical work being done seemed to be having no spiritual effect.[43] A year later the picture was very different. Although there was opposition, he was now seeing many people of different backgrounds, including Jewish people, enquiring about faith. These included an older Spanish person, a young girl who wanted to be baptised, a French mother who said 'I believe in Jesus and my sins are all forgiven', and a young Spanish man.[44] Patrick was able to form a church among Spanish and English people, with attendances on Sunday evenings of about 130 adults in one room and 70 children in another, and up to 150 who could not get into the building.[45]

Another missionary supported by the Pastors' College Missionary Association was Thomas Gillard Churcher, a student at the College in the late 1870s who, with Spurgeon's approval, went to Edinburgh to study medicine. After graduating in 1884 he worked at the Mildmay Mission Hospital, Bethnal Green, and then moved to North Africa, which was the scene of his life's work. Spurgeon strongly supported the Kabyle Mission (later the North African Mission), with which Churcher served. Together with his wife, who was a hospital nurse, Churcher pioneered medical services in Morocco (in Tangier and Fez), where he was the first European medical doctor, and in Sousse, a large city on the coast of Tunisia.[46] In the early 1890s Churcher reported that he was seeing about 100 patients a week, while superintending the Hospital, 'Hope House', and the Dispensaries of the Tangier Medical Mission. Churcher commented on the religious situation in Morocco, saying that for many people only secret discipleship was possible, since religious liberty was not a concept that was embraced. There were, he said, some secret disciples.[47] A report in *The Sword and the Trowel* in 1903 said that during his time in North Africa Churcher had treated up to 70,000 patients and that Christianity was much more favourably viewed as a result of his work.[48] In 1894 Thomas Spurgeon spoke of his father's 'holy audacity' in starting the College Missionary Association, but confessed that it was now financially precarious.[49] Two years later Charles Spurgeon called for further support.[50] In addition to ministry in North Africa, the Missionary Association helped to support missionaries in France and South America, but it did not flourish as C.H. Spurgeon had hoped.[51]

The College and Baptist world mission

Links between the College and the BMS grew closer during the later 1870s and the 1880s. T.L. Johnson, who came to the College in 1877, was assured by Spurgeon that he would have his full support in his desire to go to West Africa.[52]   In October 1878 *The Baptist* reported: 'Special farewell services to the Revs. T. L. Johnson and C. H. Richardson, who are going to Africa as missionaries, the former having been accepted by the Baptist Missionary Society and trained by them for the past two years in the Pastor's College, were held on Wednesday last week in the Metropolitan Tabernacle. There was a very large attendance, and Mr. Spurgeon occupied the chair, introducing Mr. Johnson, who delivered an interesting address upon slave life, mission work in Africa, and his

T.L. Johnson's motto "Africa for Jesus"

expectations and purposes respecting the future.'[53] After their arrival in West Africa, Mr and Mrs Johnson and Mr and Mrs Richardson spent time in Freetown, Sierra Leone, and in Monrovia, Liberia, and then settled in Cameroon, but soon after this illness struck the Johnsons. In *The Sword and the Trowel* for January 1880 Spurgeon included a letter which contained, as he said, 'a very touching account' from T.L. Johnson of his wife's suffering. The fever which she contracted led to her death. Johnson expressed his thankfulness for the support of the congregation

Letter to Mr. Johnson from Mr. Spurgeon.

at the Metropolitan Tabernacle and concluded the letter. 'Yours truly, for Africa'.[54] Johnson returned to the USA in 1881 and had a long ministry among American and English Baptists. C.H. Richardson continued to work in Bakundu, Cameroon, reporting in 1886 that he had distributed (among traders who could speak English) Spurgeon's sermons sent by Mrs Spurgeon, and that he was also translating them.[55]

Another part of Africa which was the focus of much College attention was the Congo. Two members of the Metropolitan Tabernacle, J.H. Weeks and A. Billington, who studied at the College in the late 1870s, joined the BMS Congo Mission in 1881. Both served until just before the First World War. Others from the College followed, but some died within two or three years of arriving in Africa. J.W. Hartley and Sidney Comber were among those whose deaths were mourned in the College. In April 1885 Spurgeon wrote about Comber, who was from Park Road Baptist Church, Peckham: 'All these years we have watched over this brother only to see him go to Africa and die: yet it must be right.'[56] Rather than discouraging others, the deaths acted as a challenge. At the 1885 College Conference it was reported that six College students had volunteered for the Congo. Spurgeon spoke of 'true Christian heroism' being apparent.[57] More followed later. In 1886 Australian pastors trained at the College paid tribute to the heroism of the Congo missionaries.[58] Between 1884 and 1886 twenty-one BMS recruits joined the Congo Mission, making the BMS missionary force the largest in the Congo.[59] The College was a significant contributor to this growth. Regular reports came to the College in the 1890s from the Congo and there was encouragement to read the BMS *Missionary Herald*. One Congo missionary, R.H.C. Graham, commenting in 1893 on College statistics of pastors, explained that BMS missionaries were not the pastors of the churches they planted. At this point seven former College students were in Central Africa with the BMS.[60] John Weeks helped to expose the exploitation of Africans by the Belgian authorities in the Congo. In 1907 he and Billington, together with the ten others trained at the College who were in the Congo, thanked the College and the Tabernacle for their support.[61]

China was also a country in which the BMS worked, and although some within the College constituency favoured the CIM, a number of former students served in China with the BMS. Indeed in 1887 it was reported that S.B. Drake, who after his College course had been with the CIM in China for a decade, was going back to China with the BMS.[62] He served until 1910. In the early 1890s there were eight missionaries from the College in China, some engaged in medical work and some in planting churches. Among these were two brothers, Albert and George Huntley, and in 1893 Albert reported that a church had been planted which had eighty-one members.[63] A year later Huntley reported that there had been evidence of political instability, with some rioting, but that the work of planting churches was progressing. Forty-two baptisms had taken place in June 1894, and there were by then fifteen local workers as well as foreign missionaries.[64] Six years later, however, the Boxer uprising in China brought about the first martyrdom of someone from the College: Silvester Frank Whitehouse went to China in 1888 with the CIM, returned to England and studied at the College, and then served in China for only one year when he and his wife were killed.[65] On 18 September 1900 Archibald McCaig read a telegram to the College from Baynes of the BMS announcing the massacre of Mr and Mrs Whitehouse.[66] In 1902 Thomas Spurgeon unveiled a marble tablet honouring the College's first martyr.[67] Later the College's missionary fellowship was named the Whitehouse Missionary Fellowship. When McCaig looked back in 1913 on twenty years as a College tutor, he said that he had known 300 students who had trained at the College and that 10% of these were engaged in foreign mission. Three had died for their faith.[68]

The BMS had, from its beginnings, strong connections with the Indian sub-continent. Robert Spurgeon, who came to the College from the Free Church of Scotland, Dumbarton, went to India in 1873. In the early 1880s College-trained missionaries in India – Robert Spurgeon, H. Rylands Brown, J.G. Potter, W.S. Mitchell, William Norris, G.H. Hook and R.W. Maplesden – sent united greetings to College Conference. They were joined by

George Dann and John Stubbs. Although working in different places (Madras, Agra, Calcutta and Darjeeling) they felt united. C.H. Spurgeon wanted to encourage students to think about work in India reaching English speakers.[69] This route was taken by F. Durbin, who became pastor of the English Baptist Church, Cinnamon Gardens, Colombo, Ceylon (now Sri Lanka), and H. Rylands Brown, who worked with the Darjeeling Union Church and the Anglo-Indian Evangelization Society. A College report in 1894 included news of G.H. Cook, at the Lall Bazar Chapel, Calcutta, who had baptized sixteen people. Cook mentioned the need 'to repair this old Chapel of Dr [William] Carey's'. At Cinnamon Gardens, Colombo, where T.I. Stockley was then pastor, services were held in English, Tamil and Singalese, with good numbers of British soldiers attending.[70] Stockley later had ministries in West Croydon, Jamaica and Toronto. College Conference heard from members in India in 1907 that 'the Doctrines of grace' are 'in our hearts and upon our lips as God's message of grace to a lost humanity'.[71] Links continued – in the 1950s Colin Weller, a former student, served in Ceylon, as did George Lee from the early 1960s, and Delvin Knower and Fred George, both from Sri Lanka, came to College and then took pastorates in England.

International partnerships

An increasing emphasis in the twentieth century was on mission partnerships across the world. Events were held in College – some under the auspices of the Whitehouse Missionary Fellowship - to highlight world needs. Stanley Pearce, who went to Ceylon in 1906 after his College training, served with the BMS until 1951. Another long-serving minister was William Forde, from Barbados, who came to College in 1903 and then went to Costa Rica, initially with the BMS, and served there until 1968, caring for a dozen churches.[72] In Patna State, India, F.W. Parry helped to constitute sixteen churches between 1914 and 1917. The Congo remained central. C.H. Chilvers went to the Congo with RBMU in the 1920s and Malcolm Guthrie with BMS a decade later. Guthrie then taught at the University of London. Arthur Elder went to China in 1940, and remained there until the expulsion of missionaries in 1949-52. Half the students who trained from 1939-40 to 1943-44 – Cyril Austen, Fred Drake, Walter Fulbrook, Bruce Henry, Harold Kitson and Jim Sutton – went overseas with BMS.[73] Frederick Stainthorpe and Russell Warden were among those who went later. From 1966 Fred Drake, after service in Congo/Zaire, became BMS Associate Overseas Secretary and then Overseas Secretary. In the same period Basil Amey, a student in the early 1950s, was BMS Assistant Home Secretary and Editor, and (from 1979) Assistant General Secretary, British Council of Churches. From 1959 to 1966 Donald Monkcom, at College in the 1940s, was Principal of Calabar College, Jamaica, later the United Theological College of the West Indies. Spurgeon's had strong connections with a range of BMS ministries.[74]

A new area of BMS partnership opened up in 1953. Arthur Elder, who had been born in Argentina, was interested in service in South America. The expulsion of missionaries such as Arthur and Kathleen Elder from China meant that BMS personnel and finances were available for new work. With BMS backing, the Elders went to South America in 1953 and made contact with Brazilian Baptists. Arthur Elder was invited to become pastor of a new Baptist congregation in Ponta Grossa, Paraná state. Although Southern Baptist missionaries had been in Brazil since 1881 this area had little Baptist witness. Partnership between the BMS and the Paraná Baptist Convention proved fruitful. Derek and Beryl Winter went to Brazil in 1957. In 1961 Paraná Baptists urged the BMS to send as many workers as possible and by 1965 there were eight BMS couples in Brazil. A strong Spurgeon's involvement was evident, through (for example) A. Brunton and Sheila Scott, Roy and Margaret Deller, Tony and Gill Boorne, and David and Doris Doonan, and later Derek and Joanna Punchard, Gerald and Johan Myhill, John and Maria Dyer, and Stuart and Georgie Christine. The early emphasis was on church planting, but later the contribution Derek Winter, David Doonan, Stuart Christine and others made to theological training was seen by Brazilian Baptists as crucial. In 1966 Waldemiro Tymchak was the first Brazilian to come to Spurgeon's, sponsored by the BMS. Subsequently the BMS financed others, such as Joao Garcia, to study at British Baptist Colleges, mostly at Spurgeon's. The intention was to supply Brazilian Theological Colleges with tutors, although some, like Garcia, also became involved in Brazilian Baptist world mission.[75] Stuart Christine taught at Spurgeon's from 1988-91, when the Christines returned to Brazil. From the early 1990s they have pioneered innovative social, educational and evangelistic ministries in the slums of Sao Paulo, and now pan-continental responsibility.

In the mid-twentieth century former College students were serving in Australia, New Zealand, the Caribbean, Canada, USA, South America, Africa, Malaya, and several European countries - France, Italy, Belgium, Germany, Spain, Holland, Latvia, and Russia. Australian connections were strong, with A.L. Leeder speaking in 1949 of almost fifty Australian ministers trained at Spurgeon's.[76] C.J. Tinsley was perhaps best known. Similar links existed with New Zealand. Alex Hodge was in ministry there for three decades, beginning in 1936. In the 1950s, Denzil Robertson from Calabar College, Jamaica, came to study at Spurgeon's. Canadian and American connections were fostered by pastors such as Alex McCrae, in Ontario, John Steer in the USA, and Bruce Milne, from 1984 at First Baptist Church, Vancouver. Two Spurgeon's Principals, George Beasley-Murray and Michael Quicke, moved to the USA to lecturing posts. Colin Grant, a student in the 1950s, was later Secretary of the Evangelical Union of South America. In southern Africa, C.W. Parnell, who left Spurgeon's in 1942, was General Secretary of the Baptist Union of South Africa. Others trained at Spurgeon's who served in southern Africa in the middle decades of the century included A.J. Barnard, Robert Philpott, E.B. Edwards, C. Winter, and John Jonsson, who became Principal of the Baptist Theological College of Southern Africa.

Later, Noah Pashapa came from Zimbabwe and returned to develop a remarkable ministry in Harare. Emmanuel Okewole from Nigeria, and Joao Makondekwa, from Angola, were at Spurgeon's in the 1960s. Okewole returned to Nigeria to lecture and Makondekwa was Director of the Bible School at Kimpese, Zaire, before returning to Angola and becoming General Secretary of the Bible Society.[77]

The twentieth century has seen many links between the College and the countries of Eastern Europe. Miss Von Kirchner, a Baptist from Russia who spoke at College Conference in the 1890s about the persecution of Baptists in her country, was a precursor.[78] Robert Fetler (William's brother) studied at the College from 1912 to 1915. He died during World War II after imprisonment and torture. Another Latvian, August Korp, a student in the 1920s, became the Baptist Bishop of Latvia.[79] Despite Soviet restrictions, Michael Zhidkov and Anatol Kirukhansev from Russia were able to study at the College in the 1950s. Other Russian students followed later, and Svec Stanislav from Prague studied for a short period in 1969. Some of these students became significant Baptist leaders. Several students came to Spurgeon's from Eastern Europe in the 1990s, for example Teddy and Diddy Oprenov from Bulgaria, who later led the Baptist work in Bulgaria, with Teddy as senior pastor of the central Baptist church in

Russian students in 1967.

Sofia. Others who trained at the College have fostered mission links. Vic Jackopson's 'Hope Now' mission began to serve in a range of ways in Ukraine. Clive Doubleday, the founder of Smile International, has pioneered significant evangelistic and social ministries in Albania, Kosova and an increasing number of other countries. Several of those who trained at College in the 1990s went with the BMS to Eastern Europe - Croatia, Albania and Bulgaria. Throughout the twentieth century there have been important links between the College and the countries of Eastern Europe.

There have also been connections with Western Europe. In the 1890s the leading French Baptist, Pastor Saillens of Paris, was recommending young members of his church who spoke English to study at the College. They offered to give French lessons to members and friends of the Metropolitan Tabernacle in exchange for board and lodgings.[80] Philippe Blocher from France studied in the 1930s. Later there were Dutch students, including Evert Huizing and Heinrich Stukker, both of whom commenced ministry in Holland in 1955-6. In the 1960s George Beasley-Murray, who had taught at the Baptist Seminary, Rüschlikon, travelled extensively in Europe, lecturing in many countries, including Germany, Sweden, Russia, Switzerland and Spain. Ron Goulding, minister of Haven Green, Ealing, and College

Council chairman, became Secretary of the European Baptist Federation (EBF) in1965.[81] Paul Beasley-Murray frequently represented British Baptists at BWA meetings. His speaking engagements in Europe took him to many Western and Eastern countries, and his principalship coincided with the emergence of a new Europe. Post-communist Europe offered new opportunities. From the late 1990s the College had close links with the

The International Baptist Theological Seminary

International Baptist Theological Seminary (IBTS), which moved from Rüschlikon to Prague in 1994.[82] Among those from Spurgeon's who went with the BMS to different parts of Europe, Robert and Cath Atkins and Phil and Rosemary Halliday went to France, and Mark and Claire Ord to Italy. Mark Ord has played an important part in setting up a partnership between the Italian Baptist Union and Spurgeon's. A wider European partnership has been established between the College and the International Baptist Convention (English-speaking Baptist churches in Europe and elsewhere) to assist in church-based training. In 2000, Pieter Lalleman, a Dutch Baptist minister, became the first continental European appointed to the College staff. European links continued and strengthened.

Conclusion

In 1889 there were representatives from North Africa, Congo, China, India, Jamaica, USA and Australia at College Conference and it was estimated that 168 former College students were serving abroad. In 1891 C.H. Spurgeon stated: 'The world is our parish, and our brethren are not sitting down, waiting to be called to settled charges, and comfortable incomes; but they are willing to go wherever there is an opening for preaching Christ, and gathering a church'.[83] A year later, of the seventeen students completing their College studies, over one third were going overseas – mainly to the Congo, Australia and South Africa.[84] There was a cycle of daily prayer for those serving overseas. Internationalism continued in the twentieth century. J.H. Rushbrooke, General Secretary of the BWA, stated that 'none of our [Baptist] theological colleges or seminaries in the world has been more warm-heartedly international in outlook and sympathy' than Spurgeon's.[85] A number of those trained at the College served the BMS at home – for example George Cumming and Dan Weller chaired the BMS. In 1988 the College *Record* reported on former students who were overseas. Among these were: Alex McCrae, Will McLean, and Flavio and Neusa dos Santos in Canada; John Pretlove in Texas; José de Godoi in Brazil; Lauro and Thereza Mandira, Graham Ingram and Robert Philpott in South Africa; Joe Simfukwe in Zambia; Athol Gill and Ben Richardson in Australia; Alex Hodge in New Zealand; and John Murray, a chaplain in Germany.[86] Over the next few years the global nature of the College's ministry changed somewhat, as the College community itself became more multi-ethnic and greater emphasis was placed on Europe. The appointment of David Coffey, formerly President of the European Baptist Federation, as President of the BWA from 2005, is a landmark for Spurgeon's. David Coffey, perhaps the most distinguished British Baptist of his generation, has contributed significantly to the ever-widening connections of the College.

1   C. Ray, *The Life of Charles Haddon Spurgeon* (London: Passmore and Alabaster, 1903), p. 257; B. Stanley, 'C.H. Spurgeon and the Baptist Missionary Society, 1863-1866', *BQ*, Vol. 28, No. 7 (1982), p. 320.

2   Stanley, 'C.H. Spurgeon and the Baptist Missionary Society', pp. 320-1.

3   Cited by B. Amey, *College Record*, December 1969, p. g22.

4   K.R. Manley, '"The Magic Name": Charles Haddon Spurgeon and the evangelical ethos of Australian Baptists', Part 1, *BQ*, Vol. 40 (July 2003), pp. 180-1.

5   *Outline*, 1867, pp. 95-6.

6   T.W. Hearl, 'Baptist Pioneers of St. Helena' (privately produced, 1995), p. 6.

7   *Outline*, 1868, p. 4.

8   *S and T*, April 1873, p. 149.

9   Fullerton, *Spurgeon*, p. 239.

10 A.E. Wilmott, *Greater Things* (London: Spurgeon's College, n.d.), p. 15.

11 J.A. Spurgeon, 'Report of College Studies', *Outline*, 1867, p. 29.

12 *S and T*, March 1873, pp. 128-31.

13 *S and T*, April 1873, p. 149.

14 *S and T*, April 1878, p. 189.

15 *S and T*, July 1882, p. 379.

16 *S and T*, March 1873, p. 131; April 1873, p. 149. Wigston and Blamire later joined the Brethren.

17 *S and T*, June 1878, p. 306.

18 *S and T*, June 1881, p. 306.

19 M. Sutherland, 'Downgrade down under', *BQ*, Vol. 37, No. 7 (1998), pp. 351-63.

20 *S and T*, June 1881, pp. 305-6.

21 Manley, 'The Magic Name', pp. 178-80.

22 *S and T*, June 1881, pp. 305-6.

23 *S and T*, April 1873, pp. 149.

24 *College Record*, April 1949, pp. 12-17.

25 *S and T*, January 1889, p. 44.

26 *S and T*, December 1889, p. 670.

27 F.W. Boreham, *My Pilgrimage* (London: Epworth Press, 1940), chapter 22.

28 *AP*, 1912-13, pp. 10-11.

29 *S and T*, May 1903, p. 246.

30 J.A. Stewart, *A Man in a Hurry* (Asheville, NC: Russian Bible Society, n.d.), pp. 39-40, 90-1, 104; cf. J. Wood, *Born in the Fire* (privately published, 1998). See also A. McCaig, *Wonders of Grace in Russia* (1926), held in the Spurgeon's College Heritage Room, file J2.10.

31 *S and T*, September 1879, p. 446.

32 Nicholls, *C.H. Spurgeon: The Pastor Evangelist*, p. 80.

33 *S and T*, September 1879, p. 446.

34 F. Hale, 'The Spanish Gospel Mission', *BQ*, Vol. 40 (July 2003), pp. 152-72.

35 See S. Mondello and P. Nazzaro, 'The Origins of Baptist Evangelism in Italy, 1848-1920', *American Baptist Quarterly*, Vol. 7, No. 2 (1988), pp. 110-27.

36 *S and T*, September 1880, p. 462.

37 Price and Randall, *Transforming Keswick*, pp. 52, 113.

38 *S and T*, March 1883, p. 150.

39 Murray, *Letters of Charles Haddon Spurgeon*, p. 119.

40 *S and T*, April 1881, p. 175.

41 *S and T*, January 1889, p. 44.

42 C.H. Spurgeon from Mentone, 14 December [1888], Correspondence of Spurgeon, 1863-1886, Heritage Room.

43 *AP*, 1891-92, p. 4.

44 *AP*, 1892-93, pp. 43-4.

45 *AP*, 1893-94, p. 30. He returned to ministry in England in 1899 and was later an Area Superintendent.

46 *S and T*, September 1903, pp. 456-60.

47 *AP*, 1892-93, p. 43.

48 *S and T*, September 1903, pp. 456-60.

49 *S and T*, November 1894, pp. 605-6.

50 *S and T*, February 1896, p. 84.

51 Fullerton, *Spurgeon*, p. 240.

52 Johnson, *Twenty-Eight Years a Slave*, p. 90. For background on this 'Black Atlantic' endeavour see D. Killingray, 'Black Baptists in Britain 1640-1950', *BQ*, Vol. 40 (April 2003), pp. 69-89.

53 Johnson, *Twenty-Eight Years a Slave*, p. 101, citing *The Baptist*, 4 October 1878.

54 *S and T*, January 1880, pp. 42-3.

55 *S and T*, February 1886, p. 92.

56 *S and T*, April 1885, p. 197.

57 *S and T*, June 1885, pp. 295-6. Missionaries in the period 1885-7 included J.I. Maynard and J.G. Brown.

58 *S and T*, February 1886, pp. 92-3.

59 B. Stanley, *The History of the Baptist Missionary Society*, 1792-1992 (Edinburgh, T&T Clark, 1992), p. 125.

60 *AP*, 1892-93, pp. 44-5.

61 *S and T*, June 1907, pp. 279-80.

62 *S and T*, January 1887, pp. 42-3.

63 *AP*, 1892-93, p. 45.

64 *AP*, 1893-94, pp. 28-9.

65 Stanley, *History of the Baptist Missionary Society*, p. 201. The leaders of the Boxer movement practised rites which included boxing-like gestures. In the Boxer rising twelve BMS missionaries, three missionary children, and many Chinese Christians were put to death.

66 Minutes of the College Students' Missionary Association, 18 September 1900: Minute Book, 1886-1917.

67 *S and T*, December 1902, pp. 627-8.

68 *AP*, 1912-13, p. 6.

69 *S and T*, June 1882, p. 264-5; January 1887, pp. 42-3. Robert Spurgeon's grandfather, William Spurgeon, was the brother of C.H. Spurgeon's grandfather, James.

70 *AP*, 1893-94, pp. 26-7.

71 *S and T*, June 1907, pp. 279-80.

72 *College Record*, April 1951, pp. 6-7.

73 See Stanley, *History of the Baptist Missionary Society*, pp. 392-3. Four went to the Congo.

74 For wider BMS developments in the 1990s, see chapter 9.

75 For fuller details about Brazil see Stanley, *History of the Baptist Missionary Society*, chapter 15. I am also indebted to David and Doris Doonan for information.

76 *College Record*, September 1949, pp. 4-6.

77 Stanley, *History of the Baptist Missionary Society*, p. 469.

78 *S and T*, July 1895, p. 385.

79 August Korp died in 1948, aged forty-eight. See his narrative in the Heritage Room.

80 *S and T*, August 1895, p. 447.

81 This also meant being Associate Secretary of the BWA.

82 From 1999 to 2003 Ian Randall divided his time between IBTS and Spurgeon's.

83 *AP*, 1890-91, p. 4.

84 *AP*, 1891-92, p. 5.

85 *Spurgeon's College Magazine*, Christmas 1940, p. 12.

86 *College Record*, Spring 1988, pp. 4-5.

Chapter 8: Energising evangelicalism

An article in the *Daily Telegraph* on 9 May 1879 spoke of how 'numbers of young men, inspired by the teaching of Mr. Spurgeon, went out into the villages and hamlets, preaching a crusade against indifference'. The report suggested that these preachers were looked on contemptuously by the leaders of the Church of England and coldly by the leaders of the Nonconformist denominations, yet they were warmly welcomed by the people to whom they spoke. The preachers were described as 'hot gospellers'. In spite of the disapproval they faced, said the article, they had been influential. 'Fired by the example of the peripatetic preachers and of the young disciples of Mr. Spurgeon, who, proceeding from his College, have baptised right and left the converts to their views, the old-fashioned Nonconformist minister has roused himself to greater activity, and bestirred himself to maintain the position that was, for the moment, imperilled.'[1] Earlier Spurgeon had offered his own assessment of the influence of his preachers. When R.W. Dale, the leading Congregational minister in Birmingham, suggested that Calvinism was almost obsolete apart from C.H. Spurgeon, the response from Spurgeon was upbeat. 'Among the ministers of the Baptist denomination', he contended, 'there was never greater attachment to evangelical principles than at this moment, and those principles are more or less flavoured with the Calvinism now under discussion.'[2] For Spurgeon, the task of energising evangelicalism was one that demanded a robust theology as well as involvement in the task of communicating the gospel. The theological calling has always been one the College has acknowledged.

An evangelical spirit

Spurgeon was scathing about people who lacked firm convictions. Addressing the College in 1880, he ridiculed ministers who were prepared to preach whatever the deacons wanted. 'Pray inform me', such preachers asked, 'whether the church likes a high-toned Calvinism, or prefers Arminianism?' Spurgeon compared this to someone showing an exhibition of the battle of Waterloo, and answering the question, 'Which is Wellington, and which is Napoleon?' with the reply 'Whichever you please, my little dears; you pays your money, and you takes your choice.'[3] Yet Spurgeon, although he was deeply committed to Calvinistic theology, was not narrow in his sympathies. In 1865 he welcomed to the College several Church of England supporters, as well as famous Congregational ministers in London such as Thomas Binney, of the Weigh House Chapel, and Samuel Martin, of Westminster Chapel. The speeches from these visitors exhibited, said the report, 'genial warmth towards the President of the College and his work'. Large sums of money for the support of the College were also subscribed.[4] Some students at the College in its early period were not Baptists and it was reported in 1867 that J.W. Boulding, who entered

College in 1860, had 'changed his views upon the ordinance of Baptism' and was now preaching at (the Congregational) Whitefield's Tabernacle, Tottenham Court Road. Far from condemning Boulding, Spurgeon was pleased that the church's 'deserted walls' were now 'crowded with hearers'. Two Jewish Christians who had trained at the College, J. Duckett and A. Sternberg, served with the British Society for the Promotion of the Gospel among the Jews in the later 1860s.[5]

During the 1870s Spurgeon's willingness to embrace evangelicals who differed from him became even more evident. In 1871, speaking of the eighteenth-century Evangelical Revival - he called it the 'great modern Reformation' - Spurgeon stated that although 'we, as Calvinists, gravely question the accuracy of much that the Wesleyan Methodists zealously advocated', nonetheless 'the disciples of Wesley', as well as those who followed George Whitefield, 'brought out very clearly and distinctly the vital truths of the gospel of Jesus Christ'.[6] A year later Spurgeon, who was committed to the principle of open communion (welcoming all believers to the Lord's Table, not only those baptised as believers), attended the stone-laying ceremony for the new Baptist College in Manchester, which was designed, said Spurgeon, 'for the education of ministers of the close communion section of the body'. Spurgeon commented that 'for our part we rejoice in it though we have no faith in close communion. Our brethren are faithful to the old-fashioned gospel, and are not carried away by modern thought.'[7] He also spoke warmly in 1874 of the General (Arminian) Baptists, whose New Connexion boasted John Clifford, at Westbourne Park, London, as its best-known leader. Spurgeon suggested: 'It may be said that we have gone down to these brethren [General Baptists] quite as much as they have come up to us, and this is very possible; if truth lies in the valley between these two camps, or if it comprehends both, it is well for us to follow it wherever it goes.'[8] In this period Clifford was invited to speak at the College.[9]

Danzy Sheen, one of the Methodists who studied at the College in the 1860s, found himself in many debates about Calvinism and about the mode and subjects of baptism. Sheen appreciated greatly the way Spurgeon always tried to smooth the way for him. When Spurgeon recommended Elisha Coles' *Treatise upon Divine Sovereignty* (1673), he said 'Mr Sheen, you need not get this up, as I know it is not what you like.' Sheen read it anyway, commenting afterwards that he thought *coals* should be 'put on the fire'. According to Sheen, Spurgeon once said to him and some other students: 'You see, friend Sheen, perhaps we go a little too far on the one side, Divine Sovereignty, and you a little too far on the other side, human responsibility; while the Divine mind is found in the *via media*.'[10] This might be interpreted as Sheen putting a Methodist gloss on Spurgeon's Calvinism, but in 1874 Spurgeon affirmed that the 'truth of God is wider than either of the two great systems, and that there is some truth in both of them'. This willingness to see truth in Arminianism hardly denotes rigid Calvinism. 'The party names and terms are less used', said Spurgeon, 'for which we are devoutly thankful.'[11] Does this mean that Spurgeon abandoned his robust early preaching of the Five Points of Calvinism?[12] 'We have certainly not thrown away the Five Points', he insisted, 'but we may have gathered another five, and far be it from us to deny it.' Perhaps Spurgeon's associations with Methodists had affected him; he suggested that 'if you want a free grace sermon now-a-days, you will be as likely to get it in a Wesleyan chapel as anywhere' and added that when preaching in Wesleyan chapels he found his heart often 'melted by the warm-hearted congratulations of Wesleyan friends who have gloried in the gospel which we have proclaimed'.[13] The College fostered this warm-hearted evangelicalism.

Was it the case, then, that Spurgeon became narrower in his thinking in the mid-1880s and that this helped to precipitate the Down Grade controversy? After 1883 he never returned to the Baptist Union Assemblies. His address to the College Conference in 1886 certainly struck a somewhat gloomy note. Spurgeon mused: 'Our day-dreams are over: we shall neither convert the world to righteousness nor the church to orthodoxy...I fear that both church and world are beyond us; we must be content with smaller spheres. Even our own denomination must go its own way.'[14] But later that year Spurgeon seemed to condemn any kind of sectarian spirit. Speaking in the College about unity, he argued that unity was not achieved by one church calling itself 'the Church of Christ' - whether Roman Catholic, Anglican or Plymouth Brethren. He appreciated individuals within the Brethren, but he asserted that their splits had produced 'a sect which exceeds all others in party spirit and bitter exclusiveness'.[15] Even in the first half of 1887, the year in which the Down Grade dispute erupted, a broader spirit continued to mark the College. In January 1887 the annual meeting of the Students' Missionary League - which brought together Congregational Theological Colleges (Cheshunt, Hackney and New College), the Wesleyan College, Richmond, the Presbyterian College in Queen Square, Harley House, Bow, and Regent's Park College and the Pastors' College - was held at the Pastors' College.[16] The 1887 College Conference had Charles Williams, the Baptist Union President, as one of the Conference speakers. Within a few months, however, Spurgeon withdrew from the Union.

Warnings about a theological Down Grade, especially among Nonconformists, were introduced in *The Sword and the Trowel* in articles from April 1887 onwards. Spurgeon made it clear that his concern was to uphold 'the central evangelicals truths' rather than to defend Calvinism as a system, although he believed Calvinism was of help in maintaining 'vital truth'. His struggle, he said, was against those 'who are giving up the atoning sacrifice, denying the inspiration of Holy Scripture, and casting slurs upon justification by faith.'[17] In August 1887 Spurgeon wrote: 'The Atonement is scouted, the inspiration of Scripture is derided, the Holy Spirit is degraded into an influence, the punishment of sin is turned into a fiction, and the resurrection into a myth, and yet these enemies of our faith expect us to call them brethren and maintain a confederacy with them'.[18] Increasingly Spurgeon accused the Baptist Union of harbouring people who were abandoning the evangelical faith, and in October 1887 he withdrew from the Union. In announcing this a month later he spoke of 'the wretched spectacle of professedly orthodox Christians publicly avowing their union with those who deny the faith', alleging that such Unions were beginning to look like 'Confederacies in Evil'. His own position was now one of 'independency', although 'tempered by the love of the Spirit which binds us to all the faithful in Christ Jesus'.[19]   A year later, however, he became a personal member of the Surrey and Middlesex Baptist Association, which was not in the Union. He expected considerable numbers of ministers to leave the LBA, as he had done after leaving the Union, and 'form a body and a rallying point in London'.[20] In the event, negotiations by F.B. Meyer contributed to ensuring that most London ministers trained at the College remained in the LBA.[21] The evangelical spirit most of the ministers had imbibed meant they did not want to separate from fellow-evangelicals.

The Down Grade and the College

The Down Grade, which had the potential to split the Baptist Union, has been examined in some depth.[22]   As the Union's leadership sought discussions with Spurgeon, the controversy attracted comment across the wider evangelical community. Although the Baptist Assembly, when it met at the City Temple on 23 April 1888, adopted a statement of evangelical belief, it did not satisfy Spurgeon. In the meantime the effect on College Conference - which has not been explored by historians of the Down Grade - was traumatic. In January 1888 Spurgeon commented that whatever the ministers trained at the College did over the Baptist Union, his 'hearty union with them' would be maintained.[23] The following month, however, the union was strained to breaking point. The Baptist weekly newspaper, the *Freeman*, carried a report on 10 February 1888 (a version of which also featured in the *Daily News*) about a meeting a week earlier of London College Conference ministers. About 100 had met at the College under the presidency of Spurgeon and had agreed a motion put by J.A. Spurgeon and seconded by Frank Smith that before inviting Conference members to the next Conference they should be reminded of the grounds on which the College Association was formed: '(1) the doctrines of grace, (2) believers' baptism, and (3) earnest endeavours to win souls to Christ'. The resolution said that if any Conference members had 'quitted the old faith' (those holding universal salvation were specified) they should resign. This motion was passed with five of those present dissenting, and it was agreed that the resolution be posted to members of Conference and if it was accepted then only those agreeing to it would be members of the Association in the future.[24]

Events moved quickly. A paper was sent out to all Conference members asking them to reply within a week voting 'yes' or 'no' to the London resolution. E.G.

Temple Street Classroom

Gange, minister of Broadmead, Bristol, who was a distinguished member of Conference, responded in the *Freeman*. He had, he said, received 'a circular containing certain test questions' which indicated that only those whose answers were satisfactory would be invited to the forthcoming Conference. Gange requested proper deliberation. It seemed that those who had reservations about the procedure being adopted as a result of the London resolution were not going to be able to put their case. Gange continued:

> We are to express our belief in the 'Doctrines of grace'; but those doctrines, as laid down in one of our college text-books (Elisha Cole), are to many of us, doctrines of despair and doom. Long years ago we gained emancipation from them, and refuse at any cost to put our necks under such a yoke. Then any leaning towards the 'Larger Hope' is to become an effectual barrier to our fellowship. Many of the men thus struck at have for years been successful winners of souls, and today declare that the Saviour was never so precious to them; His Cross their only hope; on His atoning sacrifice they implicitly rely; His glad Gospel they proclaim with growing confidence; and for His coming they watch and wait.[25]

It was impossible to ignore Gange. As recently as the 1885 Conference, which Spurgeon referred to as a 'holy week', Gange had delivered a powerful address on the 'Unction of the Holy One'.[26] Others supported Gange in his views. W.B. Haynes, who had studied at the College in the 1870s and was a minister at The Green, Stafford, spoke about 'this obnoxious resolution' and recalled that when Spurgeon reissued the *Baptist Confession of Faith* in 1855 he explained that it was not an authoritative rule by which people were to be fettered.[27] It appeared this had now changed.

Although only a week was given for ministers to decide about the new Conference arrangements, C.A. Davis from Reading, formerly pastor of Sion, Bradford, the leading Baptist church in Yorkshire, and now at the historic King's Road Baptist Church, Reading, contacted ministers to present a petition to Spurgeon. As he did so, Davis expressed his sorrow about developments: 'The spirit of brotherhood which has prevailed until now', he said, 'has made our Conference one of the happiest and most united associations in the world.'[28] Within a week of Davis' action, over 100 ministers had signed a protest. On the other hand, about 400 ministers returned the forms signifying agreement with Spurgeon. Tensions were growing. Spurgeon's response to criticism was that he would resign from Conference and form a new body. He was adamant that he would have no fellowship with those holding to the 'New Theology', in particular 'post-mortem salvation'. Writing to Davis, Spurgeon - who was deeply hurt by the opposition - suggested that those who were in love with 'advanced thought' had better go their own way rather than stay with an 'old fogey' like him.[29] But the ministers who opposed Spurgeon's policy over Conference insisted that they were true to the gospel. J.C. Thompson, an effective minister of Brondesbury Chapel,

London (a church with a congregation of 400), was, with C.A. Davis, particularly vocal. Thompson maintained that when he entered the College in 1873 he held 'the vital doctrines of the Gospel' - salvation by grace alone through faith in Christ - and still did. His faith in Christ's 'infinite sacrifice' led him to 'have the largest possible hope for mankind'. Crucially, he denied 'everlasting conscious torment for any created spirit for whom Jesus died.'[30]

College Conference was now divided into two camps. A letter appeared in the *Freeman* on 24 February 1888, expressing full support for Spurgeon, from fourteen ministers, plus

Archibald Brown

the College tutors, David Gracey and Archibald Fergusson, and Spurgeon's secretaries, J.W. Harrald and J.L. Keys. The ministers included several who were influential in London Baptist circles - A.G. Brown at the East London Tabernacle, William Cuff in Shoreditch, C.B. Sawday, at King's Cross, and then Melbourne Hall, Leicester, W.J. Styles, a Strict Baptist pastor at Kepple Street who had trained at the College, William Williams at Upton Chapel, Lambeth, and John Wilson in Woolwich.[31] In the same issue of the *Freeman* fourteen ministers who were Conference members, and who voiced great personal affection for Spurgeon, signed a statement opposing new tests - especially about the subject of future punishment - for Conference members. The signatories included Davis and Thompson, perhaps the prime movers, E.G. Gange, T.G. Tarn, of St. Andrew's Street, Cambridge (who had a strategic university ministry), and George Hill at South Parade, Leeds. Among the others were several London pastors. All endorsed the original Conference basis. They also affirmed: 'The inspiration and authority of Holy Scripture as the supreme and sufficient rule of our faith and practice; the Deity, the Incarnation, the Resurrection, and the Sacrificial work of our Lord; justification by faith - a faith which works by love and produces holiness; the work of the Holy Spirit in the conversion of sinners and in the sanctification of all who believe.'[32]

Discussions, claims and counter-claims continued. A College circular expressed strong opposition to Thompson's views, and for his part C.A. Davis made clear that he and his fellow-signatories did not hold post-mortem salvation.[33] The old Conference arrangements gave way to a Pastors' College Evangelical Association and all new members signed an extended statement, which was essentially the Evangelical Alliance (EA) basis of faith. In 1864 Spurgeon had resigned from the EA when it would not take his side in the 'Baptismal Regeneration Controversy' - when Spurgeon condemned evangelical clergy for using the Book of Common Prayer when they did not believe its teaching on the salvific effect of infant baptism.[34] Spurgeon was subsequently reconciled to the EA and in March 1888 addressed EA meetings at Exeter Hall and Mildmay Conference Hall on 'Fundamental Truth'.[35] He applauded the Alliance for 'calling together Christians of all denominations to bear united testimonies to the common faith', and spoke of the privilege of addressing 'vast and enthusiastic audiences'.[36] Out of about 600 members of the old College Conference, 432 agreed with the revised stipulations and joined the new Association.[37] The Down Grade created enormous tensions within the Conference community. However, Levi Palmer, who left the College in 1874 and was a strong upholder of Spurgeon at the time of the Down Grade, attended the Baptist Union Assembly in 1895 (for the first time), and wrote that 'the meetings of the Baptist Union that I have just attended prove that he [Spurgeon] did not die in vain. In all the meetings there has been visible a mighty reaction in favour of those Evangelical doctrines which C.H. Spurgeon so loved and taught.'[38] Later the College would join both the Baptist Union and also become a member of the Evangelical Alliance.

Continuing theological disputes

The process of reconciliation was not, however, a straightforward one. As Spurgeon acknowledged, those removed from the Association had found supporters, and he spoke of the split in the Conference as 'the sorest wound of all'.[39] It was much easier for him to speak out against Baptist Union policies than to be separated from those he had guided in their training and ministries. In the College's annual report for 1888-89 he spoke of his 'immeasurable grief' over the 'defections', although he added that they were not as numerous as he had feared.[40] The Association was opened up for a time to ministers who had not trained at the College - many 'pro-Spurgeon' ministers had no College training - and this brought the total of Conference members and new associate members to 546. One new member, Hugh Brown from Dublin, an outspoken figure, addressed the 1888 Conference.[41] Two years later, Spurgeon was more conciliatory, suggesting that of those who had left the Association most had 'left under misapprehension, and are personally as loyal to the old faith as those who remain with us'. He expected they would probably return.[42] Despite this more moderate tone, Spurgeon's militant approach was one of his legacies. His last Conference address, entitled 'The Greatest Fight in the World', had an immense circulation. It was posted to every minister and clergyman in Britain, and was translated into several languages.[43]

Issues that Spurgeon had raised continued to surface after his death, for example in 1896 when four members of the new Pastors' College Association resigned. Two were BMS missionaries in the Congo. One of them, J.A. Clark, who served in the Congo from 1888 to 1931, was later welcomed back into Conference. In 1896, however, they indicated that they could no longer subscribe to the Conference's article of faith concerning the inspiration of scripture ('The Divine inspiration, authority, and sufficiency of the Holy Scriptures') nor its statement on the future punishment of the wicked at the judgment. Their resignations were accepted, with the comment that their's was a strange position for BMS missionaries to take.[44]   More information about this incident emerged later. It seemed that the two missionaries believed in conditional immortality, and James Spurgeon claimed his brother had not made belief in eternal punishment a condition of Conference membership. Thomas Greenwood had apparently been inclined to a belief in conditional immortality at the time when the new Conference was started. He told Spurgeon, who (as Greenwood recalled in 1931) replied: 'That is all right, Tom; we want you; come in with us.'[45] Another example of continuing disputes about Spurgeon in College circles was a discussion in 1900 about how to interpret a 'censure' of Spurgeon by the Union during the Downgrade. E.G. Gange, then at Regent's Park Chapel, denied that Spurgeon had been censured. Archibald Brown retorted that Gange was ignorant of the deep convictions Spurgeon had held.[46] Old divisions still ran deep.

The Fundamentalist movement of the 1920s and beyond also affected the College. British Fundamentalism was never as pervasive as the American variety, but James Mountain, from Tunbridge Wells, imitated some American developments by starting the Baptist Bible Union (BBU) and by attacking the 'Modernist movement' as an agent of anarchy and Bolshevism. C.T. Cook of Tollington Park, London (later editor of the *Christian*), who had left College in 1913, supported the BBU for a time, but disliked its belligerence. In 1922 the BMS was accused by some of tolerating liberal theology and at the 1923 Baptist Union Assembly, W.Y. Fullerton, as BMS Home Secretary, spoke of the Society's loyalty to the evangelical faith. His role in avoiding a BMS split was crucial.[47] The Assembly of the following year had the potential for conflict since T.R. Glover, a liberal evangelical, was President, but it passed without difficulty. In the early 1930s, however, Glover caused problems for the College. In March 1932, Thomas Greenwood, chairman of the College Council, proposed to the Baptist Union Council that a booklet by Glover, sponsored by the Union, be withdrawn.[48] This booklet, *Fundamentals*, suggested that the atonement was a term with no standard meaning in the Bible and in the popular sense was hardly found in the New Testament.[49]   F.J. Walkey, Central Area Superintendent, with Percy Evans, negotiated a solution: it was agreed to issue another pamphlet.[50] Evans, who had become an important denominational figure, later wrote *The Saving Work of Christ*. In the same month *The Times* carried an article by Glover arguing that openness to modern thought had been secured by the Union's stand against Spurgeon during the Downgrade. Glover spoke of Spurgeon's 'rather amateur' training of ministers. Evans and M.E. Aubrey, Union Secretary, were united in indignantly refuting Glover's statements.[51]

Further problems for the College surfaced in 1957 when Eric Worstead, the Principal, made it known that he had been spiritually helped by a conference arranged by the MRA - Moral Re-Armament.[52] The Executive Committee of the College Council met on to discuss the issue, since there were doubts within the College constituency about the commitment of MRA to evangelical beliefs. The matter was also discussed with Eric Worstead. On 5 July 1957 the Executive members set out their thinking in a letter to the Council. They stated

College Group 1956 with Eric Worstead as Principal

that they believed the interest of the Principal in MRA sprang from a deep spiritual experience, they respected his sincere convictions, they held him in high regard, and they hoped the present difficulties would be overcome. The Principal's allegiance to the gospel was not in doubt, but his advocacy of MRA had embarrassed many connected with the College. The Executive's recommendation was that the Principal be asked for written assurance that he would not identify himself publicly with MRA and would write to the *Baptist Times* to say his adherence to MRA did not represent the position of the College.[53] The Council on 12 July 1957 discussed the recommendations. Eric Worstead gave assurance that he would take great care to ensure that he did not associate the College with MRA. Various opinions were expressed and it was finally agreed that Worstead would be asked if he would accept the recommendation of the Executive.[54] Over the succeeding weeks the situation was not resolved and on 13 September 1957 the Council suggested

that the Principal should resign. It was reported at the Executive on 30 September that he would do this.[55] W.H. Tebbitt, Council chairman, said of Worstead: 'We have parted from him with great reluctance but as friends.'[56]

College Group 1948-1952 Reunion in 2002

Contributions within Baptist life

Percy Evans, together with two tutors appointed in 1938, Frederick Cawley and Ronald Ward, contributed to wider evangelical scholarship, all gaining doctoral degrees for their scholarly work. Ward went on to teach at Wycliffe College, Toronto. Up until the 1950s, however, the staff published relatively little scholarly material. This pattern changed dramatically with George Beasley-Murray. He published his PhD, *Jesus and the Future*, and later his commentary on Mark 13, which was controversial for suggesting that Jesus was mistaken with regard to the exact timing of the Parousia.[57] Eschatology would remain one of his major interests. Beasley-Murray was one of the Baptist ministers who co-operated in the production of a book in 1959, *Christian Baptism*, which was a landmark in Baptist thinking about baptism. In the 1960s Beasley-Murray produced *Baptism in the New Testament* and then *Baptism Today and Tomorrow*. These writings promoted a more sacramental view of baptism and made him 'the foremost Baptist sacramentalist' in this area.[58] Other important books followed. In 1960 Charles Johnson, as College chairman, suggested that Spurgeon's had a faculty 'second to none in the Baptist denomination'. He wrote: 'The influence of the Principal grows in the denomination as well as in the wider Christian world, especially in the realm of Biblical and theological scholarship.'[59] Raymond Brown specialised in church history as well as writing several commentaries and each of the Principals who followed similarly gave time to writing.[60] Whereas before the 1950s it was unusual for the College's tutors to publish to any great extent within their own fields, by the 1990s this was the norm.

Another concern for the College under George Beasley-Murray was to link theological work with the life of the churches. At the 1971 Baptist Union Assembly Michael Taylor, the Principal of Northern College, gave an address which appeared to question traditional Christology and at the Union Council's executive in October 1971 Beasley-Murray proposed that 'this Council records its belief that the address by the Rev. Michael Taylor does not apparently do justice to the teaching of the New Testament concerning our Lord Jesus Christ'. This was defeated.[61] Frank Fitzsimmonds commented on the Union's stance at College Council and hoped that if any future statements made by the Union were unsatisfactory consideration would be given to making clear the College's position.[62] At the Union Council meeting in November the Union's commitment to orthodox Christology as expressed in its Declaration of Principle was affirmed, but the Council also agreed that 'the Union has always contained within its fellowship those of different theological opinions and emphases, believing that its claim for toleration involved tolerance and respect within its own ranks'.[63] At a special meeting of the College Council in December 1971 a resolution was passed (with one abstention) stating that the College stood in the evangelical tradition, holding firmly to the full deity and humanity of Christ. A motion critical of the Union's statement was passed by a two-thirds majority.[64] Ministers began leaving the Baptist Union, including some, such as Alec Steen (BRF Secretary), trained at Spurgeon's. George Beasley-Murray involved himself fully in the debates and at the 1972 Assembly seconded a resolution put by Sir Cyril Black, MP, asserting 'the unacceptability of any interpretation of the person and work of Jesus Christ our Lord which would obscure or deny the fundamental tenet of the Christian faith that Jesus Christ is Lord and Saviour, truly God and truly Man'. 1,800 delegates voted in favour, with 46 against and 72 abstentions.[65] Beasley-Murray subsequently wrote in the *College Record*: 'The Assembly of 1972 saw a momentous step taken, as our people responded wholeheartedly to a call to declare their faith.' He suggested that in proclaiming the faith those trained at the College should be in the forefront.[66]

Linked with theological direction was spiritual direction. A number of ministers trained at the College were members of the Baptist Revival Fellowship, led by Theo Bamber. In the later 1960s some BRF members, such as Leslie Larwood, a College student in the 1930s and minister at West Croydon, were concerned that the BRF was no longer primarily concerned with spiritual revival.[67] In the early 1970s most of the BRF's new leadership left the Union, and there was division within the BRF over the charismatic movement. However, a new group emerged within the Baptist Union which brought fresh spiritual impetus. Informal discussions in 1977 led to a meeting in February 1978 between Raymond Brown, Douglas McBain (later the London Superintendent) and Paul Beasley-Murray. After further meetings with an enlarged group, a new movement, 'Mainstream' ('Baptists for Life and Growth'), was launched. The newsletter affirmed wholehearted commitment to the Gospel 'as expressed in the Union's Declaration of Principle' and to the denomination's life and work. The early Mainstream leadership included Raymond Brown as president and David Coffey as secretary, as well as other significant denominational figures such as B.R. White, Principal of Regent's Park College. The annual Mainstream conference attracted 300-400 people and acted as a focus for spiritual renewal. It was not explicitly charismatic in its spirituality; rather it brought together those with different perspectives on renewal within Baptist life.[68] Ministers within the Spurgeon's constituency played an important part in the development of Mainstream.

Ministers trained at Spurgeon's also contributed to wider denominational affairs. In the April 1989 *Mainstream Newsletter*, the editor, Terry Griffith, who left College in 1980, spoke of Mainstream's concern for the deepening of evangelical faith among Baptists, for the rediscovery of Baptist identity and for the encouragement of mission-minded leadership.[69] A year later the Newsletter featured proposals by Nigel Wright that the Union reform its structures, engage in decentralization, and act as a resource agency.[70] During the 1980s, when Bernard Green was Union General Secretary, the Union made important advances, not least the move of the offices from London to Didcot, to a modern building shared with the BMS.[71] With the retirement in 1991-2 of Green and Douglas Sparkes (the Deputy General Secretary), David Coffey was appointed General Secretary and Keith Jones (later the Rector of IBTS, Prague) Deputy General Secretary. Coffey had pastorates at Whetstone, at North Cheam and at Upton Vale, Torquay, and his presidency of the Union and work as Secretary for Evangelism brought him to the centre of Union life. He was the first General Secretary to have trained at Spurgeon's.[72] During the 1990s a great deal of thought was given to Baptist identity. Nigel Wright's *Challenge to Change* (1991) and Paul Beasley-Murray's *Radical Believers* (1992) were both widely read.[73] Far-reaching changes in Union life were agreed. A group chaired by Nigel Wright produced a report, *Relating and Resourcing*, recommending the merging of the existing Associations and the Areas to create about sixteen regional associations, each served by a team comprising pastoral, evangelistic and other ministries, with regional ministers employed and paid locally.[74]

Changes were implemented with the hope that the Union would be more effective in mission.

Evangelical renewal

From the 1950s onwards Spurgeon's developed increasingly strong links with the wider evangelical community represented by bodies such as the Evangelical Alliance. In the 1940s and 1950s Martyn Lloyd-Jones, minister of Westminster Chapel, spoke to the Theological Students' Prayer Union at the College. This Prayer Union, to which most students in this period belonged, was connected with the Inter-Varsity Fellowship (IVF). George Beasley-Murray was involved in the wider IVF-linked Theological Students' Fellowship (TSF) and spoke at one of the TSF Conferences at Swanwick on 'Biblical Eschatology'. Beasley-Murray was aware, however, that some of his views were not entirely acceptable within conservative circles. When he produced his commentary on Mark 13 in 1957 he expected, as he put it, that 'the IVF will swear to make the angels blush'. Some were critical, but Beasley-Murray's work was acclaimed by F.F. Bruce, the foremost evangelical biblical scholar of the time. Significantly, when Beasley-Murray was appointed Principal of Spurgeon's, Douglas Johnson, IVF General Secretary, who had encouraged Beasley-Murray to become a scholar, similarly encouraged him to foster 'the great tradition of Spurgeon along with the true scholarship in these changed times'.[75] College links with the IVF (later the Universities and Colleges Christian Fellowship - UCCF) continued. In 1966-7 Bruce Milne was chairman of TSF. Chris Voke, who trained at the College and had ministries in Upper Beeding and Gillingham, was an IVF Travelling Secretary before entering pastoral ministry, as was Andrew Rigden Green, minister at Upton Vale, Torquay. Later the UCCF largely drew its personnel from independent and Anglican circles and most students in Christian Unions attended such churches, although South Parade, Leeds, which had two Spurgeon's-trained ministers, David Morris and Karl Martin, was an example of a Baptist church with large numbers of students attending.

At the same time, however, the Evangelical Alliance, which grew rapidly in the 1980s and 1990s, drew Baptists into its varied enterprises. Raymond Brown, who was EA President in 1975-6, was involved in discussions about the future of the EA in the early 1980s.[76] From then on, as the EA advanced under the leadership of Clive Calver and then Joel Edwards, each of the College's Principals and several of the tutors have been involved in EA affairs. Robert Amess, who trained at the College in the 1960s and whose ministries included Bethesda, Ipswich, and Duke Street, Richmond, became EA chairman in 1999. Later he combined this with chairmanship of the College Council. In parallel with the increasing influence of the EA was the rapid growth of Spring Harvest, an annual Easter event which by 1988 was attracting 50,000 people (having started in 1979). Spring Harvest utilised among its speakers people trained at or teaching at the College, such as Paul Beasley-Murray, Steve Chalke, Stuart Christine, David Coffey, Rachel Dutton, Steve Gaukroger,

John Maile, Stuart Murray, Michael Quicke, Debra Reid, and Nigel Wright. One-third of those attending Spring Harvest were Anglicans, one-third Baptists and one-third from other denominations.[77] Many Baptists were working pan-denominationally. An example was Steve Chalke's Oasis Trust, which cared for homeless young people, provided (in conjunction with the Spurgeon's) training up to degree level in youth ministry, and pioneered other educational projects world-wide. Christmas Cracker restaurants, which Chalke initiated, raised large amounts of money for social projects in Africa and India. Through his work in the media, and with Faithworks, his most recent major initiative, Steve Chalke became better known to the British public than any other Baptist minister in Britain.[78]

Spurgeon's has also contributed to wider ecumenical progress. In the 1960s, at a time of considerable tension among Baptists over ecumenical involvement, George Beasley-Murray chaired the Baptist Union's Advisory Committee for Church Relations (ACCR). He worked with the General Secretary of the Union, David Russell, and with two ministers trained at the College, Stanley Voke and Leslie Larwood, to seek to address the tensions. In 1967 ACCR produced a major report, *Baptists and Unity*. This acknowledged that there was probably 'no other major denomination in which there is such widespread doubt concerning the present desire and movement to recover the unity of the Church'. The report advocated continued Union membership of the British Council of Churches (BCC) and the World Council of Churches. It was presented to the Council by George Beasley-Murray, and adopted in March 1967.[79] Earlier in the year Beasley-Murray had been condemned by the Protestant Truth Society for sharing a platform with a Roman Catholic priest on the staff of the BBC, Agnellus Andrew.[80] In the 1980s Baptists were involved in consultations which led to the replacement of the BCC by new ecumenical bodies - Churches Together - which included Roman Catholics as well as Black churches. Robert Amess was involved in talks on behalf of the EA.[81] In 1989, and again in 1995, votes were taken at Baptist Assemblies supporting Baptist participation in Churches Together. David Coffey was personally supportive of ecumenical commitment, but worked for good relationships with Baptists who did not wished to be involved in ecumenism.[82] In 2003 he became Moderator of the Free Churches Group in association with Churches Together in England (CTE) - the most senior Free Church office in England.

The final aspect of the College's involvement in evangelical renewal is the aspect that has always been central: ministry. The training of men and women for ordained Baptist ministry has remained the College's core activity, but people also train for various ministries. Part-time (usually one day a week) study opportunities leading to the Cambridge Diploma in Religious Studies began in 1979, attracting large numbers of students from a variety of denominations, and from the 1990s part-time study has been through the University of Wales, leading to a certificate, diploma or degree. In 1999, for example, the College welcomed 100 new part-time students. Some go on to train for ordained ministry. Accredited courses in counselling developed under the leadership of Sheila Smith, and then Tricia McIlroy, both trained counsellors. Distance learning was discussed at College Council in 1948,[83] and in 1962 A.E. Willmott, the College Secretary, noting a lack of progress, commented: 'I believe there is a need in our denomination for the training of lay folk in Biblical, Theological and Historical subjects, either through postal tuition, or in lectures, or both.'[84] Open Learning developed in the College through distance learners studying for the Cambridge Diploma, then through the Open Theological College, and more recently under the University of Wales. The MTh in Applied Theology course, led by Peter Stevenson, who trained at Regent's Park College and had ministries in Bedford, Shirley, and Chatsworth, West Norwood, has attracted people from various denominations. While the majority are Baptists, there are also Anglicans, Salvation Army officers, some Bible College tutors, and pastors in Pentecostal and 'new' churches, reflecting the College's place within wider evangelicalism.

Conclusion

C.H. Spurgeon's concern to be a prophetic voice to evangelicals led him to take some drastic actions in the period of the Down Grade controversy, actions which ruptured relationships within the College Conference. Gradually, however, wounds healed. Thomas Spurgeon, speaking in 1901 on 'One Lord, One Faith, One Baptism', told the College Conference: 'I am as desirous as any that all the evangelical forces of Christendom should gather together.'[85] During Percy Evans' period the College drew closer to the Baptist Union. With reference to Spurgeon's own withdrawal from the Baptist Union, Evans was satisfied that the Union's constitution, since that debate, incorporated a proper doctrinal statement.[86] George Beasley-Murray and Raymond Brown were active in connecting the College with the wider evangelical world. Both contributed to the shaping of evangelicalism through writing and speaking. When Paul Beasley-Murray became Principal he addressed what was perceived to be a problem regarding the College's image. Discussions in 1985 suggested that the College needed to do more to appeal to people who no longer thought in denominational terms. In particular it needed to be represented at Spring Harvest.[87] Over the next few years this took place. Paul Beasley-Murray wanted all strands of evangelical life to be represented in College, including charismatic and Reformed. Above all, as he put it in 1988, he wanted a College which held fast to Christ and his word, and so was gladly associated with the 'conservative evangelical tradition', while also confronting common value systems in church and world - and so was radical.[88] Nigel Wright, who became Principal just over a decade later, sought to continue to stimulate the College to be both orthodox and questioning. His own thinking was outlined in 1996 in *The Radical Evangelical*. The College was now a member of the Evangelical Alliance, and thus the EA basis of faith Spurgeon advocated had been embraced by the College. In both 1855 and 2005, however, the Spurgeonic approach to evangelical faith was a radical one.

1   *Daily Telegraph*, 9 May 1879, cited by Fullerton, *C.H. Spurgeon: A Biography*, p. 228.

2   *S and T*, January 1874, pp. 49-51.

3   *S and T*, June 1880, p. 257; *All-Round Ministry*, p. 149.

4   *S and T*, May 1865, p. 229.

5   *Outline* (1867), pp. 84-5.

6   *AP*, 1870, p. 5.

7   *S and T*, December 1872, p. 531.

8   *S and T*, January 1874, p. 52.

9   *AP*, 1873-74, p. 9.

10 Sheen, *Pastor C.H. Spurgeon*, pp. 82-3.

11 *S and T*, January 1874, pp. 51.

12 The Five Points are usually summarised as total depravity, unconditional election, limited atonement, irresistible grace, and the perseverance of the saints.

13 *S and T*, January 1874, p. 52.

14 *S and T*, June 1886, p. 255-7.

15 *S and T*, October 1886, pp. 514-16.

16 *S and T*, January 1887, p. 43.

17 *S and T*, April 1887, pp. 195-6.

18 *S and T*, August 1887, p. 397.

19 *S and T*, November 1887, p. 560.

20 *S and T*, December 1888, p. 652.

21 Randall, *Spirituality and Social Change*, pp. 67-71

22 The best account is in M. Hopkins, *Nonconformity's Romantic Generation: Evangelical and Liberal Theologies in Victorian England* (Carlisle: Paternoster Press, 2004), chapters 5 and 7. See also Payne, *The Baptist Union*, pp.127-43; E.A. Payne, 'The Down Grade Controversy: A Postscript', *BQ*, Vol. 28, No. 4 (1979); Kruppa, *Charles Haddon Spurgeon*, chapter 8.

23 *S and T*, January 1888, p. 44.

24 Freeman [hereafter *F*], 10 February 1888, p. 81. It was later alleged that a number of those present had abstained, but abstentions were not counted.

25 *F*, 17 February 1888, p. 101.

26 *S and T*, June 1885, pp. 294-5.

27 *F*, 17 February 1888, p. 101.

28 *F*, 17 February, p. 113. Responses from about a quarter of the members of College Conference are held in the Heritage Room (B1.16).

29 *F*, 24 February 1888, pp. 127-8.

30 *F*, 2 March 1888, p. 137.

31 *F*, 24 February 1888, p. 129.

32 Ibid.

33 *F*, 2 March 1888, p. 137.

34 I. H. Murray, *The Forgotten Spurgeon* (Edinburgh: Banner of Truth Trust, 1973), chapter 5.

35 Evangelical Alliance Executive Council Minutes, 12 April 1888. For Spurgeon, the Alliance, and the Alliance Basis of Faith, see I.M. Randall and D. Hilborn, *One Body in Christ* (Carlisle: Paternoster Press, 2001), chapters 2 and 5 and Appendix 2.

36 *S and T*, May 1888, p. 249.

37 *F*, 16 March 1888, p. 168.

38 *S and T*, January 1896, p. 19.

39 *S and T*, March 1888, p. 148.

40 *AP*, 1888-89, pp. 3-4.

41 *S and T*, June 1888, p. 301.

42 *AP*, 1889-90, pp. 3-4.

43 Fullerton, *Spurgeon*, p. 239.

44 *S and T*, March 1896, pp. 150-1.

45 Memorandum from Percy Evans held with the minutes of the Executive Committee of the Council, 28 November 1946. A copy note of 28 November 1931 is attached.

46 *BT*, 19 January 1900, p. 45; 26 January 1900, p. 64. There were abortive attempts in 1905 and 1915 to remove any reference to the Down Grade from the Baptist Union minutes.

47 D.W. Bebbington, 'Baptists and Fundamentalism in Inter-War Britain', in K. Robbins, ed., *Protestant Evangelicalism: Britain, Ireland, Germany and America, c1750-c1950* (Oxford: Blackwell, 1990); Stanley, *History of the Baptist Missionary Society*, pp. 377-81.

48 W.M.S. West, 'The Reverend Secretary Aubrey: Part 1', *BQ*, Vol. 34, No 5 (1992), pp. 201-2.

49 T.R. Glover, *Fundamentals* (London: Baptist Union, 1931), p. 23. For the controversy, see Clements, *Lovers of Discord*, pp. 120-4.

50 Minutes of the Baptist Union Council, 7-9 March 1932; BT, 10 March 1932, p. 158; 17 March 1932, p. 175.

51 *The Times*, 11 March 1932, p. 8; *BT*, 17 March 1932, p. 180; West, 'The Reverend Secretary Aubrey: Part 1', p. 203.

52 *BT*, 26 January 1956, p. 10.

53 Letter to Council Members, 5 July 1957, from W.H. Tebbit, Chairman, and the Vice-chairman and treasurer.

54 Minutes of College Council, 12 July 1957.

55 Minutes of the Meetings of the Executive Committee and the Council on 2, 4, 10, 13 and 30 September 1957.

56 *College Record*, December 1957, pp. 11-12.

57 Beasley-Murray, *Fearless for Truth*, p. 73.

58 *The Fraternal*, July 1959, p. 4; Cross, *Baptism and the Baptists*, esp. pp. 225-7 and 235-43.

59 *College Record*, December 1960, p. 18.

60 For example, R. Brown, *The English Baptists of the Eighteenth Century* (London: Baptist Historical Society, 1986); P. Beasley-Murray, *Dynamic Leadership* (Eastbourne: MARC, 1990); M.J. Quicke, *360-Degree Preaching* (Carlisle: Paternoster Press, 2003); N.G. Wright, *Free Church, Free State* (Carlisle: Paternoster Press, 2005).

61 Minutes of the Baptist Union General Purposes and Finance Committee, 5 October 1971; cf. Peter Shepherd, *The making of a northern Baptist college*, (Manchester: Northern Baptist College, 2004), pp. 231-4. Peter Shepherd trained at Spurgeon's in the 1970s.

62 Minutes of College Council, 12 October 1971.

63 Minutes of the Baptist Union Council, 9 and 10 November 1971.

64 Minutes of a Special Meeting of College Council, 10 December 1971.

65 *BT*, 27 April 1972, p. 7.

66 *College Record*, June 1972, pp. 4-5.

67 *BRF Bulletin*, No. 91, April/June 1967, p. 1: Spurgeon's College, BRF Archive, *Bulletin* file.

68 *Mainstream Newsletter*, No. 1 (March 1979), p. 1; cf. D. McBain, *Fire over the Waters: Renewal among Baptists and others from the 1960s to the 1990s* (London: DLT, 1997), pp. 82-5, 108-14.

69 *Mainstream Newsletter*, No. 32 April 1989, p. 1.

70 *Mainstream Newsletter*, No. 35 (January 1990), pp. 2-4.

71 D.C. Sparkes, *The Offices of the Baptist Union of Great Britain* (Didcot: Baptist Historical Society, 1996), pp. 45-7.

72 *BT*, 9 May 1991, p. 7. Keith Jones trained at Northern College.

73 N. Wright, *Challenge to Change: A Radical Agenda for Baptists* (Eastbourne: Kingsway Publications, 1991); P. Bealey-Murray, *Radical Believers: The Baptist Way of Being the Church* (Didcot: Baptist Union, 1992). *Radical Believers* has been translated into a number of other languages.

74 *Relating and Resourcing* (Didcot: Baptist Union, 1998), pp. 10-15; BT, 26 March 1998, pp. 1 and 8.

75 Beasley-Murray, *Fearless for Truth*, pp. 74-6, 91.

76 Randall and Hilborn, *One Body in Christ*, pp. 280-1.

77 *BT*, 22 April 1982, p. 1; 10 May 1984, p. 15; 27 March 1986, pp. 1, 2; P. Beasley-Murray, 'Renewal in Baptist churches', *Renewal*, No. 130 (March 1987), pp. 27-8; McBain, *Fire over the Waters*, p. 135.

78 From 2003 he was minister of Christ Church and Upton Chapel, Lambeth.

79 See G.R. Beasley-Murray, *et. al., Baptists and Unity* (London: Baptist Union, 1967).

80 For this see Beasley-Murray, *Fearless for Truth*, pp. 135-9.

81 Minutes of the Executive Committee of the Evangelical Alliance, 22 June 1988.

82 *BT*, 18 May 1995, p. 3.

83 Minutes of College Council, 4 March 1948.

84 *College Record*, June 1962, pp. 2-4.

85 *S and T*, May 1901, pp. 211-14.

86 Minutes of College Council, 15 December 1938.

87 Papers with Executive Committee Minutes, 19 June 1985.

88 *College Record*, Spring 1988, p. 3.

Chapter 9: Conclusion

This book has had as its focus the aspects of the vision that C.H. Spurgeon had for the Pastors' College and the way in which that vision has been worked out. Many other aspects of Spurgeon could be studied - his amazing preaching ministry, his theology, his prolific writing, his spirituality, or his concern for social issues, as expressed in the extensive ministry of his Orphanage at Stockwell and also in his political commitments, such as his opposition to war. While all these areas of Spurgeon's life and ministry are connected to one another, each needs separate attention and so they have not figured in this book. It is important to see, however, that Spurgeon's vision for training was shaped by his overall concept of ministry. It is this which is reflected in the phrase 'a school of the prophets'. The training was for practical purposes, with the intention of producing effective pastors. From the beginning, as David Bebbington puts it, there was 'no attempt to compete for scholarly distinctions or to turn theology from a vocational into an academic subject'.[1] The significance of the College as a place of vocational training has continued to be recognised. In 1963 George Beasley-Murray referred to a book that had been written, *Encounter with Spurgeon*, in which the author, Helmut Thielicke, a leading German theologian, suggested that the most important result of Spurgeon's work was the founding of the Pastors' College.[2]

It is clear that from very early on in his ministry in London Spurgeon wanted to send people out in mission. In a sermon preached at New Park Street Chapel on 5 August 1855 he said: 'I want to find some in my church, if it be possible, who will preach the gospel.'[3] Spurgeon encouraged activity, commenting: 'Whenever I meet a young Spurgeonite - and I do not know where it is possible to go without meeting one - I find him bouncing about like an india-rubber ball …whatever he may have in his knapsack, he goes marching on.'[4] After Spurgeon's death, the planting of new churches, which had been a crucial element in Baptist growth, became less central, but George Beasley-Murray's principalship was marked by a passionate concern for those trained at the College to be evangelists. In 1968 he wrote: 'Evangelism and the care of souls have been as the life blood of Spurgeon's College from the days of its founding. Everybody knows that Spurgeon was the pastor-evangelist par excellence …Spurgeon's only published lectures, the famous *Lectures to my Students*, were devoted precisely to the dual themes of evangelism and pastoral instruction.'[5] From the 1980s the College put in place courses particularly aimed at offering training in mission, now seen much more explicitly as involving both evangelism and social action. In post-Christian Western Europe the stress in College training on ministers as those leading the church in mission is likely to increase.

It has also been a priority for the College that students develop in their spiritual lives. In the College Spurgeon felt that he could speak 'without restraint' about both the highs and lows of spiritual life and of ministry. In speaking to the students he believed that it was right to give an 'autobiographical tinge', arguing that 'my own experience, such as it is, is the most original contribution which I can offer'.[6] The classes led by tutors opened up opportunities for spiritual as well as theological discussion.[7] Daily praying together was also crucial. One student in the early twentieth century, William Fetler, from Latvia, spoke of his

William Fetler

own spiritual journey in terms of 'three conversions' - putting his faith in Christ, receiving 'an endowment of the Holy Ghost', and becoming concerned for those who were spiritually lost.[8] In the history of the College, spiritual life has also been fostered through on-going links, for example through College Conference. An early Conference was spoken of by those present as an occasion which 'both overwhelmed and refreshed us'.[9] In the future it is likely that the development of character and of spirituality, alongside gaining knowledge and skills, will assume even greater importance. The College is taking seriously the need for pastors to be engaged in ministry which has attentiveness to God at its core. The pattern of formation that has been used in recent years at Spurgeon's has included daily worship, reflection groups, one-to-one 'Personal and Spiritual Development' interviews, and the availability of the help of the College chaplain - usually a designated member of the College staff.

The College has also integrated training in the churches with training in the College in a way that reflects Spurgeon's original vision. The College has existed to serve the churches. Against the background of debates about 'unemployed' ministers, Spurgeon argued against understanding 'the ministry of Christ's gospel to be a Trade Union' and contended that the churches needed more, not fewer ministers.[10] Increasingly the College has contributed not only to local church ministries but also to the wider resourcing of ministry. Within the Baptist Union and the Associations, the involvement of those trained at Spurgeon's is considerable. In 2004 David Coffey was Union General Secretary, Paul Goodliff, who had been Central Area Superintendent and then Regional Team Leader,[11] was Head of Ministry, with Ian Millgate in ministry support within the Department, and Derek Allen was Head of the Department for Research and Training in Mission, with Nick Lear and Terry Jones as Mission Advisers and Wale Hudson-Roberts as Racial Justice Co-ordinator. Regional Baptist Associations also had a number of Spurgeon's trained ministers serving them - Phil Jump as Team Leader in the North West, John Claydon as Team Leader in the North, with John Singleton in the team, Norman Tharby as Team Leader of the South East Partnership, with David Hall as part of the team, and Nigel Coles as Team Leader in the West of England. Other regional team members were Helen Wordsworth (Central), Ian Bunce and Richard Soar (Eastern), Kumar Rajagopalan (London), Jeremy Brown (South West) and Bill Allen (Yorkshire).[12]

Part of the resourcing from the churches has been financial. The College report for 1870 noted that the College had no Trust Funds. Spurgeon attempted to raise money so that students who had no resources of their own could come to College, but students had to agree that if the money was not forthcoming they had no legal claim on Spurgeon.[13] In fact many students from poor backgrounds and with very basic education were accepted and trained. Spurgeon was convinced that, as he put it, useful ministers 'spring from all ranks, that diamonds may be found in the rough, and that some who need most pains in the polishing, reward our labour a thousandfold'.[14]

Evening classes - again largely financed through Spurgeon's efforts - and a book fund for 'workers with slender apparatus' (a famous lecture with this title refers to lack of books, not ability) were ways by which opportunities were opened up for training. The wish to broaden possibilities for training has continued, although circumstances have changed. The College was less likely in the twentieth century

Temple Street Library

to be training people from deprived areas than had been the case in the nineteenth century. Nonetheless, financial support was still needed. In 1945 the College made an appeal for £10,000 because it was seeking to give training to a very large number of applicants who had come out of the Forces. Gifts were received not only from Baptists but also Anglicans, Brethren, Presbyterians and others. The amount that was needed was given.[15] This kind of need continues.

Although Spurgeon looked for diversity within the College, neither he nor the College Principals up to the 1950s could have envisaged the kinds of developments that would take place in the later twentieth century as Britain became an increasingly multi-ethnic country. As well as becoming ethnically diverse, the College community has also moved away from being a community largely made up of single men. Nor could the influences of ease of travel and of new technology have been foreseen. These have enabled a great deal of new opportunities. The MTh course in Applied Theology and more recently the MTh in Preaching have attracted people able to come to London from other countries for the

College photo 2003

intensive weeks of teaching and to keep in contact through e-mail. Most of the MTh in Applied Theology students are involved in some form of ministry in the UK, but others are from Denmark, Sweden, France, Italy, Israel, Australia and the USA - an example being the Mennonite Bishop of Los Angeles. In 2002 the College developed a link with the Ghana Baptist Theological Seminary which enabled students in West Africa to gain access to the course, and about thirty are engaged in MTh study. This is a strategic investment in leadership training in the African context. The students in France and Italy tend to be British missionaries working there.[16] Technology has also enabled the growth of Open Learning. Keith Neville was Open Learning Development tutor from 2000 to

Ghana MTh Students with Peter Stevenson

2003, before returning to pastoral ministry, and Debra Reid then became the director of Open Learning. At the end of 2004 over 300 students were working towards University of Wales awards by open learning, with courses offered through CD-ROM.

The 'distance' element in the story of the College is, however, not new. In 1892 a College report spoke of how students had travelled great distances to come to College: within Britain they had come from places as far distant as Wick and Redruth, while considerable numbers had come from different parts of Europe, and many had found their way to the College from all round the world.[17] Students have also gone across the world. In 1881 Spurgeon remarked: 'The earnest action of the College Missionary Society has been a source of great joy to me; for above all things I desire to see many students devoting themselves to foreign work.'[18] With the loss of Christian identity within Britain, the distinction between home and overseas mission has become less significant, but global mission is still strategic. In the 1990s those trained at Spurgeon's were involved in strategic roles within the BMS (which became BMS World Mission) and the Union. Derek Rumbol, who was at Spurgeon's in the 1950s and then served in Zaire, was BMS Regional Secretary for Africa from 1985 to 1997. In the 1990s, John Passmore, a student at Spurgeon's in the 1970s and then a BMS missionary in Bangladesh, became a BMS Regional Secretary, first for Europe and then for North Africa and Asia. David Kerrigan, who left College in 1991 and served in Sri Lanka, became BMS World Mission's Director of Mission in 1999. The BMS opened the International Mission Centre in Birmingham (formerly St Andrew's Hall, Selly Oak), and Alan Pain, of Sutton Coldfield, became Centre Director. In 2001 Phil Halliday, who had been at College in the 1980s and had served with the BMS in France, became BMS Regional Secretary for Europe.

Finally, the College has contributed to wider evangelicalism. Spurgeon spoke of a theological contribution that had, he believed, to be made. He maintained in an address in College in 1874 that evangelical doctrines had to be upheld. Yet he also warned: 'Don't go about the world with your fist doubled up for fighting, carrying a theological revolver in the leg of your trousers.'[19] The College has sought to contribute to theological engagement through MTh courses in Biblical Studies and Doctrine, and these have attracted Baptists and those from other denominations. Many of those who have trained at the College and are now in Baptist leadership are also involved in the Evangelical Alliance. As examples of other contributions to evangelical life, T. Wilkinson Riddle and Bruce Hardy both became editors of the *Christian Herald*. Internationally, Reginaldo Kruklis from Brazil, who studied at the College in the 1970s under a BMS scholarship, was later President of the Haggai Institute, training leaders across the developing world. The College has, however, never seen itself as offering a general theological education for those entering varied spheres of evangelical life. In this respect it differs from a College such as the London School of Theology (formerly London Bible College). Spurgeon's and LST have at times shared teachers in common, and Peter Cotterell and Peter Hicks, on the LST staff, trained at Spurgeon's. Lecturers from Spurgeon's, LST, Oak Hill (Anglican) Theological College and All Nations Christian College meet each year for a day conference. The desire to engage in rigorous theological education within an evangelical framework links Spurgeon's, LST, and other Bible Colleges, but Spurgeon's is committed to seminary rather than general College training.

What about the broader trends for the future? All the areas that have been examined and that stem from Spurgeon's own vision still appear to be relevant. However, the Christian world of the twenty-first century, at least in Britain, is increasingly post-denominational, with people easily moving between denominations. A number of those who have left Spurgeon's have ultimately joined other denominations or groups. Paul Beasley-Murray examined the data concerning those who trained at the College in the period 1955 to 1985 and found that of the 406 who left to serve in Baptist churches only 268 remained in this sphere of ministry.[20] Some Baptists joined new church groupings. Nick Mercer, who was in Baptist ministry after leaving College and was then Vice-Principal of London Bible College, became a high Anglican. On the other hand, some who enter Spurgeon's from other backgrounds come into Baptist life. It is significant that in the 1989 survey of the College, although the student body was predominantly Baptist only 25% of the students came from a Baptist background.[21] In the early 1990s the College launched an MTh in Baptist and Anabaptist studies (later entitled Radical Free Church Movements) to seek to address issues of history and identity. Nigel Wright, the College Principal, observed in 2002 in *New Baptists, New Agenda*, that it was difficult in the great majority of British Baptist churches to find more than a few people who saw themselves as 'cradle' or 'pedigree' Baptists. This created an opportunity for a new agenda for Baptists. In terms of crossing over traditional denominational boundaries there was freedom, but Wright noted that this involved an indifference to denominational values. It was against a pervasive post-denominational background that Baptist churches in Britain had to forge a fresh identity.[22]

This issue is a challenge for the College. Increasingly the approximately 200 people who are in College each week studying at undergraduate level are from a variety of denominational backgrounds. Although many students who come to College from non-Baptist backgrounds remain in their own denominations, some decide to become Baptists. One recent phenomenon has been the move of some students from new church streams into Baptist life, perhaps in part because a number of the streams that emerged in the 1970s have lost momentum, with some having split and others having closed. There are certainly new opportunities for Baptists in the twenty-first century. Attendance at Baptist worship (in Baptist Union and non-Union churches) rose from 270,900 people in 1989 to 277,600 in 1998.[23] But it is probably true that people are looking for reality in Christian experience and practice rather than a denominational label. Perhaps it is precisely here that the Spurgeonic perspective is relevant. In 1901 Thomas Spurgeon, speaking of his desire to maintain a distinctive Baptist witness, linked water baptism with the 'the baptism of the Spirit', which he saw as an experience of 'the Spirit's overwhelming power'.[24] A College which gives attention to ministry formation, evangelistic training, spiritual development, serving the churches, enabling people to flourish, encouraging international vision and seeking evangelical renewal stands in an authentic tradition as 'a school of the prophets'.

College Library and Chapel 1958

1   Bebbington, 'Spurgeon and British Evangelical Theological Education', pp. 219-20.

2   *College Record*, December 1963, p. 4.

3   Spurgeon, *Autobiography*, Vol. 2, p. 142.

4   Fullerton, *Spurgeon*, p. 236.

5   *College Record*, December 1968, p. 4.

6   Spurgeon, *Lectures to my Students*, Introduction, p. v.

7   Rogers, 'Outline', *Outline* (1867), p. 14.

8   *S and T*, 1911, p. 780.

9   *S and T*, May 1874, p. 240.

10 *AP*, 1890-91, p. 4.

11 Baptist Union reorganisation from 2002 meant that Areas and Associations were replaced by larger Associations. Paul Goodliff was among the Area Superintendents who became regional ministers of the new Associations.

12 *Baptist Union Directory*, 2004-5 (Didcot: Baptist Union, 2004).

13 *AP*, 1870, p. 17.

14 *S and T*, June 1881, pp. 302-3.

15 *Annual Report*, 1945, p. 3.

16 I am grateful to Peter Stevenson, the College Director of Training, for this information.

17 *S and T*, June 1892, p. 280.

18 *S and T*, June 1881, p. 304.

19 *S and T*, March, 1874, pp. 101-5.

20 P. Beasley-Murray, *A Call to Excellence* (London: Hodder & Stoughton, 1995), p. 2. Beasley-Murray found that 25% of those trained at Spurgeon's left ordained ministry.

21 *BT*, 21 December 1989, p. 10.

22 N.G. Wright, *New Baptists, New Agenda* (Carlisle: Paternoster Press, 2002), chapter 4.

23 *BT*, 16/23 December 1999, p. 5.

24 *S and T*, May 1901, pp. 213-14.

The Falkland Park Mansion
Home of Spurgeon's College since 1923
(Appendix 1)

[Text adapted from the booklet Forward in Faith: Spurgeon's College in South Norwood *produced in 1998 to celebrate the 75th anniversary of the College's move to South Norwood Hill in 1923]*

In the early days of the College classes were first conducted in the private home of the Congregational minister, George Rogers, of Albany Road, Camberwell. In 1861 the College moved to rooms in the newly built Metropolitan Tabernacle at Newington Butts, the area popularly known as 'The Elephant and Castle'. By September 1874 new purpose-built premises had been opened in Temple Street, behind the Tabernacle, to house the rapidly growing numbers of students. However there was no residential accommodation for students and they lodged in private houses.

By the early 1920s the College had outgrown its premises in Temple Street. Also it was felt that the community would benefit if accommodation could be offered on site. Therefore in 1921 the College Council appointed a committee to look for a house suitable for a residential college. In 1922 Mr Charles Hay Walker offered to give his house, Falkland Park, and some of the surrounding land in trust to the College in memory of his wife, Fanny. This offer was gladly accepted and the College moved to its new premises in 1923. The vestibule just inside the entrance doors of the main house contains a tribute to Mrs Hay Walker whose desire it had been for the house to come to Spurgeon's College.

The Falkland Park mansion, built in 1890, was only half a mile from Spurgeon's former home 'Westwood'. Spurgeon's house has long since been demolished and a school, Westwood Language College for Girls, now stands on the site in Spurgeon Road off Beulah Hill. In Victorian times the whole area around the Crystal Palace and Beulah Spa became particularly fashionable. The wealthy were encouraged to move from low-lying central London with its infamous 'smog' to the bracing air of the leafy suburb of Upper Norwood. Many large Victorian houses, for example those in Church Road, still stand and show what a wealthy area it must have been.

Although the house and estate to which the College moved was called 'Falkland Park' after Admiral the Hon. Plantaganet Pierrepoint Cary, Viscount Falkland, in fact Admiral Cary himself never lived in the property (despite claims in 19th and 20th century brochures and local histories, and even 'official' Spurgeon's College publications, that he did). In actual fact he died in 1886, four years before the house was built. Admiral Cary had lived at a neighbouring house, the Georgian mansion Grangehurst (sometimes described as Grange Hyrst) which had belonged for many years to his wife's family, the Mauberts. After Admiral

Cary's death his nephew inherited the estate but, as he could not afford to run it, sold out to a Mr Thomas McMeekin, a retired tea planter.

Mr McMeekin, who did not wish to live in the low rambling house, decided to build a new mansion on the estate, some 100 metres to the south of Grangehurst, and named it Falkland Park. The house was finally completed in the early 1890s. The great house itself was 350 feet above sea level and was designed in the Renaissance style, with a frontage finished in Portland stone, the remaining having white Suffolk brick facings. There were 28 bedrooms each with magnificent views, 6 reception rooms, and the drawing room was over 30 feet long with an ornate ceiling. The grounds covered 30 acres. Flower gardens skirted the woods and a path through the dense trees led to a rhododendron avenue 300 feet in length, adjacent to which was a rustic garden and ornamental lakes. The huge conservatory was cruciform in shape, containing a climbing vine, an acacia tree, Cape pelargoniums, fuchsias and a fernery. There were seven hot houses, one of which was 75 feet by 25 feet. These houses contained rare tropical and semi-tropical plants and over 3000 orchids. Also there were tomato, melon and cucumber houses, and a kitchen garden of one and a half acres with fruit trees, two peach houses and three vineries.

Falkland House was once described as 'A Garden of Eden in Norwood', in a remote world of its own, set apart and little known by the local residents. Records show that Mr McMeekin brought with him his own servants from Scotland and he employed virtually no local labour.

Unfortunately Mr McMeekin and his family lived at Falkland Park for a relatively short time. Apparently he was forced to sell the estate when his tea ships were reported lost at sea resulting in severe financial difficulties. According to sources, these same tea ships eventually came into port, but too late to prevent the sale in the late 1890s. The property was purchased by Mr and Mrs Charles Hay Walker around 1900.

Two sale catalogues in the College's archives, one for c.1900 and one for c.1912, give a fascinating glimpse of what life in the mansion must have been like. A series of photographs show the beautifully furnished rooms, the magnificent conservatory, glass houses, stables, cottages and a 'model hand laundry'. No-one is quite sure why the house was advertised for sale in 1912 (there is a large sale board on display in the Heritage Room). In the event the Hay Walkers did not sell the property but remained as owners for another ten years. During World War I the house was apparently requisitioned for military purposes and the gardens were sadly neglected. Photographs of the grounds in 1923 show a wilderness. It is a tribute to the College's gardeners over the years that the grounds have been restored.

The main entrance to the Falkland Park estate was formerly nearer the summit of South Norwood Hill and the original lodge can still be seen on the corner of Grange Hill. The carriage drive was over 800 ft in length and was bordered by shrubberies. The current drive became the main entrance when the College moved to the property in 1923. Early in World

War II the ornamental wrought iron gates were requisitioned leaving only bare pillars at the entrance.

There are several features in the main house which are of special interest today. In the Entrance Hall the stained glass window is particularly significant. Originally a magnificent Victorian window was in place, as can be seen in early photographs of the house, but this was blown out in World War II. It was replaced by a rather plain window which contained a small version of the College's emblem bearing the words 'Et teneo, et tenor'. Apparently some years later a lady who wished to remain anonymous suggested that this should be replaced with something rather more impressive so that the College's emblem could actually be seen. As a result of this suggestion a new window was designed and put in place in Summer 1972, paid for by the generosity of 1st Baptist Church, Tulsa, Oklahoma. The same anonymous lady mentioned above offered to pay for a smaller version of the window and this can now be seen in the Main Library

The Entrance Hall also contains the Honours Boards which list all the College's Principals and Tutors, Presidents and Chairmen since it was founded in 1856.

To the right of the entrance to the Student Lounge, formerly the mansion's dining room, is a marble plaque which commemorates the College's move to Falkland Park in 1923. The College's main dining room, in which portraits of former principals hang, was the Billiard Room and its extension, through which one walks to reach the newer parts of the College, was the mansion's Library. The steps down into the link passage originally led to a huge conservatory. The link passage was added in 1964 to join the Library and the rest of the College to the main house.

The Main Library was built in 1937, originally a separate block, and was designed to bring all the College's library books into one large room. Previously the books had been scattered in class rooms throughout the old building. The stained glass was added in 1972 at the same time as the window in the Entrance Hall. Inside the Library is a plaque honouring P.W. Evans, Principal from 1925-1950, in whose memory the Library was considerably enlarged and expanded in the early 1950s.

The large lecture room opposite the Main Library, the current Reference Library (built as a games room and converted to the Ref. Library in 1981) and the study bedrooms on the two floors above, were built in 1963 with the opening ceremony taking place in 1964. The lecture room contains a frieze showing C.H. Spurgeon lecturing to his students in the Temple Street building.

The corridor from the Reference Library towards the Chapel leads to the Cloister studies area, known originally as 'The Pilgrim's Way'. The rooms along this corridor, originally student study bedrooms and now studies for the teaching staff, were part of a building project begun in 1951 which culminated in the opening of the College Chapel in 1957 following a Centenary appeal. Members of the Southern Baptist Convention were most generous with their financial support and it was George Sadler, Secretary of the Foreign

Mission Board for Africa, the Near East and Europe, who laid the foundation stone for the Pilgrim's Way in 1951.

The Chapel, at the far end of the College complex, was designed to reflect the essential simplicity of a typical nonconformist meeting house. On the wall of the Chapel vestibule facing the main doors is a bas-relief in bronze, provided by the churches in the Central Area of the Baptist Union in memory of F.J. Walkey, a former Chairman of the College Council. Also in the vestibule is the original pulpit from the Primitive Methodist Chapel in Colchester where Spurgeon was converted. Above the vestibule is the Heritage Room which houses a wide range of items, including books, manuscript letters, newspaper cuttings and portraits, relating to the life and work of Spurgeon. An exhibition about his life can be seen in the glass display cases. In a further display case there are a number of early Bibles which were bequeathed to the College by A.H. Philpot and his family. Mr Philpot was a long-standing member of the College Council and a generous benefactor to the College.

Just outside the doors of the Chapel vestibule is a large bronze statue of Spurgeon. This originally stood in Baptist House in Southampton Row, London but was transferred to the College in 1992 when the Baptist Union moved to its new headquarters in Didcot. The cross on the exterior of the Chapel over the entrance was given in memory of C. Cameron Wallace, a student of the College, who was killed while serving as a Chaplain in the forces in World War II.

The above provides a very brief insight into the College on its present site. For more detailed information, see the following:-

Spurgeon's College Record (1940 onwards in the Reference Library)
M. Nicholls, *Lights to the World: A History of Spurgeon's College, 1856-1992* (Harpenden: Nuprint, 1994) (in Library and Heritage Room)
A.E. Wilmott, *Greater Things: A Popular History of Spurgeon's College c. 1965* (in Library)
G. Simmons, 'A community within a community', Open Univ. project (in Heritage Room - cupboard B)

Judy Powles
Librarian

Spurgeon's College – ownership and finances (Appendix 2)

In January 2000 a letter was received by the Principal, Michael Quicke, which set in train a series of events that would eventually lead to a historic moment in the life of Spurgeon's College. To discover its significance we need to go back to 1922.

When the fine country house, then known as Falkland Park, was given to the College in 1922 by the Hay Walker family, a trust was set up to 'Hold land and premises in South Norwood Hill intended to be occupied by Spurgeon's College.' The Hay Walker family appointed the trustees and so was formed the Falkland Park Trust. In the declaration of trust Spurgeon's College was allowed to occupy the premises as long as they wished to do so and so long as the College was conducted in a manner which accorded with the Statement of Doctrine as set out in the trust deed. Among those original trustees are found names of people who appear elsewhere in this book; Graham Scroggie being just one such name.

This situation did not change for almost 80 years. Trustees came and went, but essentially the Falkland Park Trust held the land and premises and held the College to account for its doctrinal position.

So it was that the letter was received by Michael Quicke. The Chairman of the Falkland Park Trust, Derek Warren, was inviting the College to consider a merger. At subsequent meetings between the two parties, it was considered that, after 80 years, the College was in a position to manage its own affairs and, as long as doctrinal standards were maintained, the Falkland Park Trust would no longer exist.

The timing of the letter coincided with changes in governance that the College was considering and this seemed to be a confirmation of the way forward. The changes would now include the merger with the Falkland Park Trust.

In April 2002 the College registered as a company limited by guarantee and in February 2003 a Charity Commission Scheme was published transferring the properties and land formerly owned by the trust into the name of Spurgeon's College. For the first time in its history, the College owned the premises it occupied.

Whilst the College is just half a mile from where C. H. Spurgeon lived, he did not come here, at least as far as we know. However, he would have understood the need for sound financial management of the College. For many years the work of the College was supported by the Metropolitan Tabernacle as its own but the move to South Norwood Hill meant that the College must now stand on its own feet. It had always been Spurgeon's intention that no student be turned away from training for the ministry on the grounds the person could not find the fees demanded. However, this placed a heavy strain on Spurgeon personally. In the Pastors' College Report of 1885-6 Spurgeon writes, 'I am deeply grateful to those who have found the money during the past year. I am equally in need of their assistance now. The Lord will not leave his servant, nor allow his cause to flag for lack of silver and gold. To me the inevitable care and labour are incessant, and it would be too great a strain if I had difficulty in procuring funds.'

In the Trustees' Report of 1891-2 in which they had to report the death of Spurgeon and the loss of two of its oldest tutors, they go on to say that 'the Trustees confidently ask for a continuance of the financial support accorded to this College in the past, without which they will they will be unable to supply the needs of the Institution.'

In a letter to College Conference dated January 1st, 1901, the College 'Remembrancer', Walter Hackney, urges members to be generous in their support of the College. He writes, 'A crisis of great importance has arisen in the affairs of the College. The present financial support being quite inadequate for maintenance, it is imperative that fresh and permanent resources should be discovered and retained.' It was the Metropolitan Tabernacle fire in 1898 that so affected the College finances. This crisis meant that the priority of the church was the rebuilding and, whilst the College remained high in the church's affection, it could not sustain the level of support from previous years. Other permanent means of financial support had to be found.

It is interesting to note, in view of comments made earlier in this book concerning the ways Spurgeon raised finances, that the letter continues, 'The Annual Supper no doubt will still supply perhaps £1,500.' When the total expenses of the College were £7,000 the Annual Supper raised a significant proportion of the income needed. The letter urged the College Conference to help raise £2,000 per annum. These amounts seem small to us at the beginning of the twenty-first century but in today's money they probably need to be multiplied by 100. At the conclusion of the letter, Hackney states that the work of the College must not even come into danger of discontinuance. That he was writing such a letter implies there was such a danger.

One would expect with such an illustrious founder the College would never be in want of money, but the evidence of the 1901 letter and the accounts over the years seems to suggest otherwise. The truth seems to be that Spurgeon always found it less of a challenge to raise funds for his orphanages than he did for the College. Deficits seem to have been the order of the day. Hardly any accounts that I have examined during the research for this Appendix show a surplus. Now this could mean a number of things, not least a serial lack of proper financial management. But I think it is necessary to look deeper for the real cause. As hinted at earlier, the College has always taken the line that students should not be expected, necessarily, to meet the full cost of their training. Time after time I have found that student fees written off at the end of the financial year equate to the deficit incurred by the College. In more recent times it has become impossible for the level of student fees to cover the full expenditure of the College.

Our current College Chairman, Robert Amess, has expressed the view that God keeps the financial situation as it is for it drives us to rely fully on divine providence and also remain close to the churches we serve.

Without wishing to blind readers with still more figures, the latest published accounts for the year ended 2003 showed an operating deficit of £121,890. Student fees received amounted to £549,173 whilst the total expenditure of the College was £1,094,612. In other words, fees covered a fraction over 50% of the total expenditure. As it is, each full time student was paying between £4,500 and £7,500 in fees to attend College. To raise fees to cover the full cost of running the college would mean doubling these amounts.

Such an increase is not sustainable. So how does the College manage? In just the same way that Spurgeon managed by seeking support from individuals, churches and charitable trusts. To maintain the work of Spurgeon's College requires a staggering £21,000 per week. We are so grateful to all those who support the College. In 2003 we launched the Personal Membership Scheme which is known as 'Ten' from the College motto et teneo et teneor. We sought a partnership with donors who were willing to pay £10 per month in return for a closer involvement with the College. Over £18,000 per annum is now raised in additional funds to the College. Equally important over the years has been the amount of legacy income received. We are always encouraged by those people who make provision in their wills for the work of the kingdom to continue after their death.

Churches have always been generous to the College. Many support students through College at great sacrifice by their members and they are not always easily identified and thanked. A large number of churches continue to donate to the College each year, recognising the need to partner with Spurgeon's College in the preparation of Christians for mission and ministry. This gives us the opportunity to express our gratitude to every person who has helped train the next generation of church leaders. We are also grateful to the Particular Baptist Fund for their financial support of this book and to A E Simmons Limited who have given unstinted assistance throughout this project.

Paul Scott-Evans
Business Manager

Selected index of people